SHOULD I OR SHOULDN'T I?

DRAWING TRUMPS

Marc Smith

An Honors Book from Master Point Press

Honors Books is an imprint of Master Point Press. All contents, editing and design (excluding cover design) are the sole responsibility of the authors.

Master Point Press
214 Merton St. Suite 205
Toronto, Ontario, Canada
M4S 1A6
(647) 956-4933

info@masterpointpress.com

www.masterpointpress.com
www.bridgeblogging.com
www.teachbridge.com
www.ebooksbridge.com

ISBN: 978-1-77140-159-3

Cover Design: Olena S. Sullivan/New Mediatrix

2 3 4 5 6   20 19 18 17

Contents

Introduction

The old story tells of two derelicts meeting under the Arches on the Embankment. One says to the other, "Didn't you used to play high stakes rubber bridge?"

"Yes," replies the second man, "but I never learned to draw trumps and I lost everything. Did the same thing happen to you..."

"Oh, no," answered the first bum, "I always drew trumps, and that's what led to my downfall."

The moral of the story, of course, is that your results will improve significantly by identifying those deals on which you should draw trumps and those on which you should not do so.

I have read numerous books on declarer play, and most of them seem to contain hand after hand illustrating the exceptions to the norm. My teaching experience, though, suggests that what most players really need is practise at those more mundane deals that crop up day after day. Indeed, many of the hands you will encounter in these pages require little more than counting your tricks.

Not that all of the deals here are 'easy': what would be the point of reading a book if you could already solve every problem? Some of the deals are more difficult, particularly if you have not seen the position before. Hopefully, though, having followed the logic behind the analysis of those problems here, you will then be able to come up with the winning play when you encounter similar situations at the table.

The deals here can mostly be solved by straightforward planning. In fact, forget I used the word 'planning', since even that seems to frighten people. Instead, let's simply call it 'thinking'.

If you want to test yourself as we go, cover the E/W cards and decide how you would play before reading on. At the end of each chapter, you will also find some quiz hands.

Enjoy!

M.S.

This book is dedicated to the memory of two of my former bridge partners who are sadly no longer with us. Both were not only excellent bridge players, but also wonderful human beings. They may be gone, but neither will ever be forgotten by anyone lucky enough to have known them.

To both Peter Czerniewski and to Jane Preddy I would like to say: "Thank you, it was a real pleasure".

M.S. 2016

Chapter 1 – "Should I Draw Trumps?"

The simple answer to the question is: "Probably, yes". On the majority of deals played in a suit contract, the best play is for declarer to draw trumps as soon as possible. Far more contracts fail because declarer does not draw trumps quickly than because he does so when he should not do so. At the risk of repeating myself then, let me over-emphasize this point right at the beginning: **"On most deals, you should draw trumps immediately"**.

Of course, every beginner quickly realizes that there are plenty of exceptions to this 'rule' (which is why I can write a whole book on the subject). We'll meet the most common exceptions later, but for now just remember that they are called 'exceptions' for a reason.

The winning line of play on most of the deals you will come across at the table is straightforward: draw trumps, set up side-suit tricks, cash winners, take ruffs and claim your contract. The objective is to recognize the exceptions but otherwise to follow that basic formula.

Always remember too, that you chose to play in a suit contract for a reason: **"the trump suit belongs to the declarer"**. Of course, the defenders have the opening lead so they may choose to begin the trump-drawing process by leading the suit. Indeed, there are still some players out there who think they should lead a trump whenever they cannot think of anything else to lead! Whether you take advantage of this usually-misguided notion by continuing to draw trumps or not, though, will generally be up to you as declarer.

Whether you are playing in a suit or in notrumps, it is imperative that you make some sort of plan before you play that first card from dummy. In this opening chapter we will look at how you should actually go about making that plan. The first step in a suit contract is to start by asking yourself one simple question: **"If I draw trumps, will I have enough tricks for my contract?"**

Let's start with some excitement – a grand slam. Cover the E/W cards and decide how you will play:

```
                    ♠ 8 6 4 2
                    ♡ J
                    ◇ A K Q 4
                    ♣ 9 8 7 2

♠ 7                                           ♠ 10 9 3
♡ Q 8 7 6 5 4 3        N                       ♡ 10
◇ 8               W         E                   ◇ 10 9 7 5 3 2
♣ Q 10 5 3             S                       ♣ K J 6 4

                    ♠ A K Q J 5
                    ♡ A K 9 2
                    ◇ J 6
                    ♣ A 6
```

West	North	East	South
—	—	—	1♠
Pass	4♡	Pass	5♣
Pass	5◇	Pass	5♡
Pass	6◇	Pass	7♠
All Pass			

You bid unopposed to Seven Spades via a splinter bid and an exchange of cue-bids. West leads the ◇8. How do you set about making all thirteen tricks?

Let's count the losers in the long trump hand (South) – two hearts and one club. Perhaps your immediate reaction is that dummy's singleton means that you can ruff the two heart losers. That leaves you with just a club loser to deal with, and that can be thrown on dummy's third high diamond.

Bidding and making a grand slam is always a thrill, so you quickly win the opening lead with dummy's ◇A, cross to your hand with the ♡A, and lead one of your heart losers, ruffing in dummy. Disaster — East overruffs! He returns a diamond and West ruffs. Now comes a third round of hearts. You ruff forlornly in dummy, but East overruffs with the ♠9. You manage to make the remaining tricks but your grand slam has gone three down. What foul distribution. What went wrong?

Let's try counting those losers again – two hearts and one club. How can we dispose of those three losers? Dummy has three diamond winners, but the ◊J in your hand is also a winner, which means that two of your losers can be discarded on dummy's high diamonds. Remember to ask yourself: "Do I have enough tricks if I draw trumps?" Let's count winners now – five trumps in hand, four diamonds, two high hearts and the ace of clubs comes to twelve. This means that you will still need to ruff one heart in dummy to bring your total to thirteen, but is there any rush to take that ruff?

Win the opening lead in your hand with the jack of diamonds (to avoid blocking the suit) and immediately lay down a high trump. When both defenders follow, you now know that you can afford draw all of the missing trumps and still have one left in dummy to ruff your last heart loser.

Having drawn the rest of the defenders' trumps, scoring the remaining tricks will then be plain sailing: grand slam bid and made.

The small slam on our next deal may look straightforward, but there are still some pitfalls to be avoided:

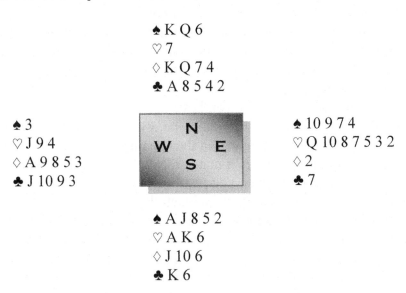

```
                     ♠ K Q 6
                     ♡ 7
                     ◊ K Q 7 4
                     ♣ A 8 5 4 2

   ♠ 3                   N              ♠ 10 9 7 4
   ♡ J 9 4           W       E          ♡ Q 10 8 7 5 3 2
   ◊ A 9 8 5 3           S              ◊ 2
   ♣ J 10 9 3                           ♣ 7

                     ♠ A J 8 5 2
                     ♡ A K 6
                     ◊ J 10 6
                     ♣ K 6
```

You quickly reach Six Spades and West leads the ♣J. How do you plan to make twelve tricks?

There are only two obvious losers. You cannot avoid conceding a trick to the ace of diamonds, so the question is how to dispose of your losing heart. You have obviously noticed dummy's shortage so perhaps you decide that you can simply take care of your heart loser by taking a ruff? For many declarers, that is as far as their planning would go, and with fatal consequences.

Take a look at the defenders' hands. Can you see what will happen if you win the opening club lead with dummy's ace, cross to a top heart in your hand, and ruff your losing heart in dummy?

You will be able to cash dummy's king and queen of spades, but there will then be no safe route to your hand in order to draw East's remaining trumps. If you try to get back to hand with a diamond, West will win and give his partner a ruff in one of the minors. If you attempt to cross in clubs, East will ruff, play a diamond to his partner's ace, and get a diamond ruff to put you two down.

"Well, that was a frightfully unlucky distribution, partner."

Many declarers would then go on to the next deal bemoaning their bad luck and never realizing that the slam could, and should, have been made. Let's go back to trick one and ask the essential question – "Do I have enough tricks if I draw trumps?"

Counting tricks, you can see five trumps in hand, the A-K of hearts and the A-K of clubs on top – that's nine. You can also establish three diamond tricks by force, by knocking out the ace. That brings your total to the required twelve. So, let's win the opening lead and draw trumps: not quite so fast – you have not quite finished your thinking yet. There is one more question to be asked before you play to trick one – where are you going to win the opening club lead?

If you wondered, "Does it matter?" you need to take a second look. Remember that in the plan you just made, you counted three diamond tricks. Are you sure that you can reach the long diamond winner once you have set it up? Suppose you win the opening lead with dummy's ace of clubs, draw trumps in four rounds, and then lead diamonds. If the defenders hold up their ace of diamonds until the third round, your twelfth trick will then be stranded in an entry-less dummy. Your only possible late entry to dummy is the ace of clubs, so you must be careful not to waste that card at trick one.

Having counted that you have twelve tricks AND made a plan for cashing them all, you are now ready to play. Win the opening club lead in your hand with the king, draw trumps, and then lead diamonds until a defender takes his ace. Nothing can now stop you from throwing your heart loser on dummy's fourth diamond and the slam is yours.

It is worth mentioning one final point of technique here. In the description of the play in the previous paragraph, I simply said 'draw trumps' and 'lead diamonds'. In both cases, though, it is important that you play the cards in those two suits in the right order. Let's look at that trump suit in isolation:

♠ K Q 6

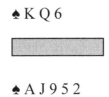

♠ A J 9 5 2

When you draw trumps here, you should play dummy's king and queen on the first two rounds of the suit. If you play the ace or the jack on either of the first two rounds of trumps, you block the suit and risk getting stuck in dummy with an enemy trump still at large. (Yes, on this occasion you would survive because you have a heart entry to your hand, but you will not always be so endowed.)

Getting used to cashing suits without creating a blockage is just a good habit to get into. Note also that it does not matter which honors are in which hand. The spade suit could just as easily have been:

♠ K J 6   ♠ A K 6

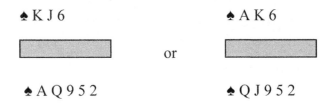

                         or

♠ A Q 9 5 2   ♠ Q J 9 5 2

Do these three spade layouts look different?

Yes, they do, but in practical terms they are identical. In each of the layouts, you have four touching honors and each of those honors is therefore of equal value. What is important is that you cash the honors in the hand with short trumps first in order to avoid blocking the suit.

This concept comes up repeatedly and it is an important one to understand, so let's look at a second example – the diamonds on the deal above.

◇ K Q 7 4

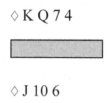

◇ J 10 6

Once again, you need to start by first playing the honors from the short suit (this time, your hand).

To see why, suppose you lead the ◇6 to dummy's king and then play a low diamond back to your jack. West can now win his ace and play a second round of clubs, removing your outside entry to dummy. You are left with two diamond winners, the ten and the queen, but you will not be able to get to dummy to enjoy the second of these.

If, instead, you start by leading the ◇J and (if that holds) continue with the ◇10, it matters not how the defenders' diamonds are divided, when they take their ace, nor what they do next. Whatever happens, you will have a diamond winner in dummy on which to discard your heart loser and, if needed, an outside entry to reach that winner.

This diamond suit is another example of a layout that can appear in different guises:

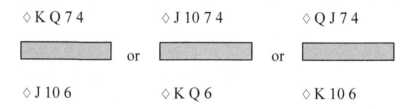

◇ K Q 7 4	◇ J 10 7 4	◇ Q J 7 4
◇ J 10 6	◇ K Q 6	◇ K 10 6

These diamond layouts may look different, but the principles are the same as we saw with the spade suit above. Your touching honors are all of equal value. In each case, you should start by leading the honors in the hand with the shorter holding first. Not doing so risks blocking the suit.

The urge to take apparently cheap ruffs in dummy can be a difficult one to overcome. Let's see how you cope with temptation on another slam hand:

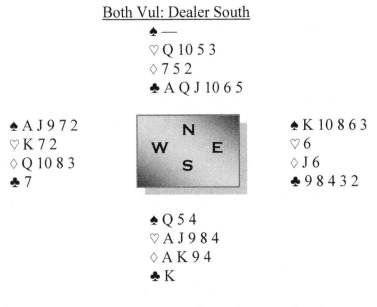

Both Vul: Dealer South

```
              ♠ —
              ♡ Q 10 5 3
              ◊ 7 5 2
              ♣ A Q J 10 6 5

♠ A J 9 7 2           N          ♠ K 10 8 6 3
♡ K 7 2         W          E     ♡ 6
◊ Q 10 8 3            S          ◊ J 6
♣ 7                             ♣ 9 8 4 3 2

              ♠ Q 5 4
              ♡ A J 9 8 4
              ◊ A K 9 4
              ♣ K
```

West	North	East	South
—	—	—	1♡
1♠	3♠	4♠	6♡
All Pass			

Although the opponents manage to elevate the bidding to the 4-level on the first round, your partner's jump cue-bid shows a shortage in spades and agrees hearts so you quickly reach slam.

West opens the defense with the ♣7.

How do you play?

If you start by counting losers in your hand, you'll see two diamonds, three spades and perhaps a trump too. That seems like an awful lot when you are in a slam contract, so your first inclination may be to reduce that number quickly by ruffing spades in dummy.

Let's see how the play might go: win with the king of clubs and ruff a spade. Lead a diamond to the ace and ruff a second spade. Now you try to cross back to hand via the trump finesse, but West wins with the

13

♡K and returns a second trump, East discarding a club. When you next cash one of dummy's top clubs, throwing your last spade, West ruffs. He exits with a spade, which you can ruff in hand, but you still have two diamonds to lose. Oops! Three down.

Let us now go back to the beginning and ask the all-important question — "If I draw trumps, will I have enough tricks for my contract?"

Even if you have to lose a trick to the ♡K, you can count four trump tricks in hand. The ace-king of diamonds makes six. You already have one club trick and there are five more club winners in dummy, which seems to bring your total to twelve. Let's just check – can you reach those club winners after trumps are drawn? Clearly, the only possible entries to dummy are in trumps, but that is okay so long as the trumps split no worse than 3-1.

Let's play it through mentally before doing anything: win with the ♣K, cash the ♡A and (assuming both defenders follow suit) continue with a second trump. What can the defenders do?

If West holds up the ♡K, you will simply win in dummy and cash winning clubs, discarding losers. Eventually, someone can ruff in with the king, but there will still be a trump in dummy to get back to the winning clubs.

Alternatively, if a defender wins the second round of trumps with the king and his partner shows out, you can ruff the spade continuation and draw the outstanding trump with the queen, keeping the lead in dummy so that you can cash the clubs.

Whatever happens, you will have no problem amassing twelve tricks – slam made!

On the deals we have looked at so far, declarer risked being seduced into ruffing at the wrong time by the lure of cheap tricks. Judging when to take your ruffs is vital.

Another way of making easy tricks is via a successful finesse. Take a look at just the N/S cards on the next deal and decide how you would play Four Spades on the lead of the queen of clubs:

```
                    ♠ J 5 3 2
                    ♡ J 7 2
                    ◇ 8 6 4
                    ♣ A 8 6

♠ 4                  N                    ♠ A 10
♡ K 10 6        W         E               ♡ Q 9 8 5 4 3
◇ K 10 9 3 2         S                    ◇ 5
♣ Q J 10 2                                ♣ K 9 5 4

                    ♠ K Q 9 8 7 6
                    ♡ A
                    ◇ A Q J 2
                    ♣ 7 3
```

When this deal occurred at the table, declarer saw that he had only two entries to dummy, the ♣A and the ♠J. After winning the first trick with the ace of clubs, he therefore 'took advantage' of the chance to take a diamond finesse, planning to use his trump entry to later repeat a winning finesse.

Looking at the full deal, you can see that this was not declarer's lucky day. The diamond finesse lost to the king and West returned a diamond for his partner to ruff. The trump ace and a further loser in clubs then put the game one down.

Declarer here failed to ask the important question — "If I draw trumps, will I have enough tricks for my contract?" Let's count – you can make five trump tricks in hand after driving out the ace, and three aces bring the total to eight. You can also establish a second diamond trick by force with the queen-jack and an extra trump trick can be made by ruffing the fourth round of diamonds in dummy. That adds up to ten, which is what you need, so you should set about the task of drawing trumps immediately.

The point is that you do not need to take winning diamond finesses playing this deal in Four Spades. You can afford to lose a trick to the diamond king. Having ascertained by simply counting to ten that you have enough tricks by drawing trumps, that is exactly what you should set about doing.

So, win the ace of clubs at trick one and immediately play a trump. Suppose that East rises with the ♠A and switches to a diamond. Can you put your hand on your heart and say that you would not finesse? As you can see, taking the diamond finesse whilst there is still a trump outstanding will leave you with the same egg on your face as our original declarer.

Instead of finessing, you should go up with the ace of diamonds and draw the defenders' last trump. Only then can you lead the queen of diamonds to drive out king and establish your second winner in that suit. Playing in this simple fashion, you will lose one trump, one diamond and one club and the game will be made.

Notice that if you had somehow bid these cards to Five Spades, the original declarer's line of play would be absolutely correct. Needing to make eleven tricks, the answer to the question "If I draw trumps, will I have enough tricks for my contract?" would have been "No". In that case, it would be clear that you need to find the king of diamonds onside, and it would be correct to utilize dummy's club entry in order to take the diamond finesse even though you had not drawn trumps. The situation is similar on our next deal:

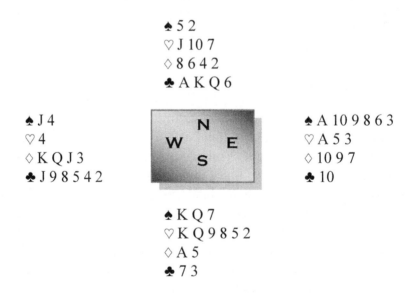

```
                    ♠ 5 2
                    ♡ J 10 7
                    ◊ 8 6 4 2
                    ♣ A K Q 6

♠ J 4                                      ♠ A 10 9 8 6 3
♡ 4              N                         ♡ A 5 3
◊ K Q J 3    W       E                     ◊ 10 9 7
♣ J 9 8 5 4 2      S                       ♣ 10

                    ♠ K Q 7
                    ♡ K Q 9 8 5 2
                    ◊ A 5
                    ♣ 7 3
```

You bid unopposed to Four Hearts and West leads the ◊K.
How do you play?

Did you spot the opportunity to dispose of your diamond loser on dummy's clubs before the defenders could regain the lead?

I'm afraid that the Bridge Gods were in a mean mood when they distributed the defenders' cards on this deal: if declarer tries that then East ruffs the second round of clubs and cashes a diamond. With two aces still to lose, the contract fails by a trick.

A simple count of your tricks should lead you to the winning solution – five hearts, three clubs, one diamond and one spade add up to ten, which is what you require. Immediately set about drawing trumps and you will make your contract.

Yes, it is unfortunate that the club suit breaks so badly, but declarer's primary duty is to ensure the safety of the contract. Trying to make an overtrick is an afterthought that should only be considered once the contract is safe.

Declarer here should play a trump at trick two, allowing the defenders to win with the ace and cash a diamond trick. There would then have been only one further loser, the ace of spades. Declarer's third spade can be discarded on dummy's club suit after all the trumps have been drawn.

Quiz Hands

1.
    ♠ K 7 5 4
    ♡ Q
    ♢ K J 10 7 2
    ♣ K 7 3

    ♠ A 6 3 2
    ♡ A 6 4 3
    ♢ Q 9 5
    ♣ Q 6

West leads the jack of clubs against Four Spades. You play low from dummy and East follows with the ♣8. How should you play?

2.
    ♠ —
    ♡ 8 6 3 2
    ♢ 9 5 2
    ♣ A K Q J 10 3

    ♠ K 10 6 5 2
    ♡ K Q J 10 4
    ♢ Q 6
    ♣ 5

West leads the ♢J against Four Hearts. East wins the ♢K, cashes the ace and plays a third diamond which you ruff. How should you play?

3.

♠ Q 10 3
♡ 10 8 5 4 2
◊ 7 3
♣ K 10 4

♠ K 8 6 4
♡ A 7
◊ K Q 8 4
♣ Q J 6

You open with a 15-17 One Notrump. Your partner transfers to hearts and everyone passes. West leads the ◊9 to his partner's ace, and East returns the ◊J which you win. How should you play?

4.

♠ 10 4
♡ A K 6 3
◊ A J 4
♣ K Q 10 5

♠ A 7 3
♡ 9 5
◊ 8 7 6 3 2
♣ J 8 3

West opens the bidding with a weak Two Spades and your partner doubles for takeout. This lands you in a rather unappetizing Three Diamonds against which West leads the ♡J. How should you play?

1.
```
              ♠ K 7 5 4
              ♡ Q
              ◇ K J 10 7 2
              ♣ K 7 3
```

```
♠ Q 9                              ♠ J 10 8
♡ K J 8 5 4        N               ♡ 10 9 7
◇ 8 3         W         E          ◇ A 6 4
♣ J 10 9 4         S               ♣ A 8 5 2
```

```
              ♠ A 6 3 2
              ♡ A 6 4 3
              ◇ Q 9 5
              ♣ Q 6
```

West leads the ♣J against Four Spades. You play low from dummy and East follows with the ♣8. There are three obvious losers – two minor-suit aces and at least one trump. You must therefore assume that the trumps will break 3-2.

Many players would see the singleton in dummy and immediately set about taking ruffs, but playing the hand through mentally should alert you to the futility of this approach. Let's see what will happen: win the ♣Q, cash the ♡A and ruff a heart. You then play a diamond to your queen, which wins, and ruff a second heart. Now what?

Actually, no matter what you do next you can no longer make the contract. If you cash the top trumps, the defenders will duck the second round of diamonds, leaving you with no entry to the long cards in that suit and thus no discard for your heart loser. Alternatively, if you continue without drawing trumps the defenders will score more than one trump trick by ruffing the third round of diamonds.

Trying to score extra tricks by ruffing hearts here is a red herring. Yes, you do need ONE heart ruff, but it is when you take that ruff that is crucial.

Remember to ask: "If I draw trumps, will I have enough tricks?" Let's count: three trump tricks in hand (assuming an even split), four diamond tricks (after knocking out the ace), one club trick already made, the ♡A, and one heart ruff with dummy's long trump – that adds up to ten.

Notice that we have counted four diamond tricks. As usual when you counting tricks in a side suit, you must check that you will be able to reach those long tricks. Here there is only one route to dummy late in the hand (assuming the defenders hold up the ◇A) – by taking a heart ruff AFTER you draw trumps and knock out the ◇A.

Win the ♣Q at trick one, cash the top spades, then play diamonds. The defenders can take their three tricks but no more. You will ruff one heart in dummy and discard the other two on dummy's long diamonds. Ten tricks and contract made.

2.

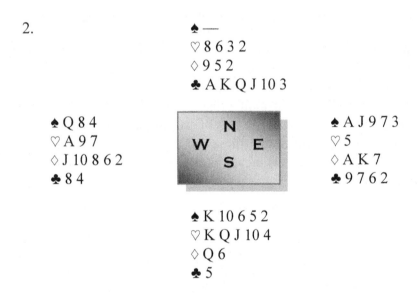

                ♠ —
                ♡ 8 6 3 2
                ◇ 9 5 2
                ♣ A K Q J 10 3

♠ Q 8 4   ♠ A J 9 7 3
♡ A 9 7   **N**   ♡ 5
◇ J 10 8 6 2   **W**   **E**   ◇ A K 7
♣ 8 4   **S**   ♣ 9 7 6 2

                ♠ K 10 6 5 2
                ♡ K Q J 10 4
                ◇ Q 6
                ♣ 5

You bid unopposed to Four Hearts. West leads the ◇J to his partner's king. East continues with the ◇A and a third round of diamonds, which you ruff.

As usual, start by asking the question — "If I draw trumps, will I have enough tricks for my contract?" This is an easy one to count – four trump tricks in hand after knocking out the ace (assuming that trumps split no worse than 3-1) and six club winners in dummy. As on the previous deal, though, the key is to ensure that you can reach dummy's long suit once the defenders' trumps have been extracted.

It is certainly tempting to start by ruffing a spade in dummy, and many players would do exactly that. Doing so, though, opens the door for the defenders to cut you off from dummy's wonderful club suit. After taking your spade ruff, you play a heart to the king (which wins). Now what are you going to do?

If you play another trump now, West wins and plays a spade, forcing you to ruff with dummy's last trump. With only clubs left now you try to discard your remaining spade losers but West ruffs the third club to put the contract one down. Alternatively, if instead you ruff a second spade before playing the second round of trumps, West wins and plays a club. Oh dear!

Instead, you should simply set about forcing out the ace of trumps as soon as you gain the lead. You are now left with two entries to dummy – one in clubs and one in trumps via a spade ruff – and the defenders have no way to remove them both before you finish drawing trumps.

The sad thing is that taking a spade ruff on this deal can never gain even a single trick. It is a total illusion. You have already lost two diamonds and must lose to the ace of trumps too, so you can never make more than 10 tricks, and those ten can be made without a ruff. Although ruffing a spade can never gain a trick, doing so can lose your whole contract.

3.

♠ Q 10 3
♡ 10 8 5 4 2
◇ 7 3
♣ K 10 4

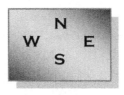

♠ A 9 5
♡ K J 9
◇ 9 6
♣ A 8 7 5 2

♠ J 7 2
♡ Q 6 3
◇ A J 10 5 2
♣ 9 3

♠ K 8 6 4
♡ A 7
◇ K Q 8 4
♣ Q J 6

You open the bidding with a strong notrump and your partner transfers to hearts. Everyone passes and there you are in a somewhat inelegant spot! Although you do not often see such contracts in books, they are relatively common at the table and most inexperienced players find them tricky to handle.

West leads the ◇9 against your inglorious Two Hearts. East wins with the ace and returns the jack of diamonds to your king. How do you play?

A quick count of losers tells you that with three aces missing you can afford to lose only two trump tricks. If the hearts split 4-2, you can never avoid three trump losers but, if the suit breaks 3-3, you may be able to crash the defenders' high trumps together.

When your trumps are poor, playing the suit at every opportunity can prevent the defenders from scoring their big trumps separately. On this deal, if you do anything other than lead trumps immediately you will go down, so start by cashing the ♡A and continuing with a second round of trumps.

West wins this trick with the ♡J and plays a low club (hoping that his partner holds the ♣Q). Note that you need to get to dummy urgently in order to play a third round of trumps, but you also need to preserve a club entry to your hand for later, so which card you play from dummy on this trick is crucial. In fact, you must play the king. (If East captures this trick with the ace, you can then unblock an honor from your hand, promoting the ♣10 into an entry.)

When the king of clubs wins, you can play a third trump, felling the ♡Q and the ♡K together. Whatever the defenders now do, you will be able to force an entry to your hand with the ♣Q-J in order to discard dummy's spade loser on your remaining high diamond. (You see now why it was essential to get the ♣K out of the way earlier.) Your only other loser is the ♠A.

4.

♠ 10 4
♡ A K 6 3
◇ A J 4
♣ K Q 10 5

♠ K J 9 6 5 2
♡ J
◇ Q 5
♣ 9 7 4 2

♠ Q 8
♡ Q 10 8 7 4 2
◇ K 10 9
♣ A 6

♠ A 7 3
♡ 9 5
◇ 8 7 6 3 2
♣ J 8 3

Partner quite reasonably makes a takeout double of West's weak Two Spade opening bid, but this is not your lucky day and you once again find yourself in a rather unappetising contract: Three Diamonds.

West leads the ♡J.

How do you play?

Counting tricks (three trumps, three clubs and three winners in the majors) confirms that you have chances provided trumps behave. A count of losers confirms this: there are two spades, one club and two trumps, but the second spade loser can be discarded on dummy's long club.

First, though, you must deal with the trump suit. You are prepared to lose two trump tricks but you cannot afford to lose three. You have, though, been forewarned of the danger: when someone opens with a pre-emptive bid in one suit and then leads a different side suit, their lead is more often than not a singleton.

If you mess around on this deal you will allow West to get a ruff with his short trump holding. Win the opening heart lead and immediately play ace and another trump. West wins with the ◇Q and switches to the ♠6, East playing the queen. As you are fairly sure that spades are divided 6-2, it is vital that you hold up your ace on the first round and then win the spade continuation.

(If you win the first round of spades, East will be able to win the
♣A, draw dummy's last trump, and lead a spade for his partner to cash
two tricks in the suit. By ducking the first spade, though, you leave
West with no entry.)

You can now set about driving out the ♣A. Your only other loser
will be East's second big trump. Contract made.

Chapter 2 – Playing for ruffs, or not

A major advantage of playing in a suit contract is that you can often score additional tricks by ruffing. However, you are always going to make tricks with your long trumps, whether you ruff with them or simply cash them. What this means is that: **"In most cases, you do not gain a trick by ruffing in the long trump hand."** This may be the most important sentence in this whole book – learn nothing else and you will still have improved your play, so go back and re-read it until you are sure you will remember it.

Playing in a 4-4 or 5-5 trump fit, you can add to the number of trump tricks you make by taking ruffs in one hand or the other. As we saw in the previous chapter, though, such ruffs can often wait until after you have drawn trumps.

It is when your trump fit is uneven, 5-2, 5-3 or 6-2 for example, that you are most likely to be able to score an extra trick or two by ruffing before drawing the defenders' trumps.

Dummy will generally be the 'short trump hand', and if you can score one (or more) of those short trumps in addition to the long trumps in your hand you will usually augment your trick tally.

Our first deal is fairly straightforward, but there are still dangers lurking in the shadows:

♠ K Q 4
♡ 6 5
◇ K 7 3 2
♣ 8 6 4 2

♠ 7 2
♡ Q J 10 8 4
◇ Q 10 8 4
♣ A 10

♠ 8 6 5
♡ 9 3
◇ J 9 6
♣ J 9 7 5 3

♠ A J 10 9 3
♡ A K 7 2
◇ A 5
♣ K Q

West leads the trump deuce against your contract of Six Spades. How would you play?

Let's count losers – one club and two hearts. You cannot hope to avoid losing to the missing ace, so you will need to dispose of the heart, and the obvious way to do this is to take two ruffs in dummy.

Where should you win the opening lead? In the previous chapter, I stressed the importance of playing honors from the short holding first in order to avoid creating a blockage. Does this mean that you should win the opening lead with one of dummy's high trumps?

To do so here would be to take an unnecessary risk. You can see what will happen if you win the opening lead with dummy's ♠K, cash the top hearts from your hand and then ruff the third round of hearts with dummy's ♠4. East will overruff and return a trump. Not only will East have scored a trick with a low trump but, with no more trumps in dummy, you will also have to lose a heart trick later (as well as the ace of clubs) — two down.

The trumps in your hand are strong enough that you can afford to take your ruffs with dummy's high trumps. Play low from dummy and take the opening lead in your hand. Now cash the ♡A-K and play a third heart, ruffing in dummy.

How are you now going to get back to your hand to take your second heart ruff?

You cannot afford to lose the lead yet: if you play a club, the defense will take their ace and play a second round of trumps, leaving you with a heart to lose at the end. Instead, you must re-enter your hand in diamonds, so perhaps you cross to the ◊A to lead your last heart and ruff with dummy's lone remaining trump.

All that remains now is to get back to your hand to draw the defenders' outstanding trumps. Should you play a club or cash the ◊K and ruff a diamond back to hand?

Actually, it is now too late to be asking this question. Did you spot East discarding diamonds when you took your two heart ruffs in dummy? If you cash the ◊K now he will ruff. If you play a club, West will win with the ace and give his partner a diamond ruff.

The problem of how to re-enter your hand after ruffing with dummy's last trump is one that needs to be considered earlier in the deal. After ruffing the first heart in dummy, you need to cash the ◊K and then play a diamond to your ace. After taking your second heart ruff, you can then safely return to hand with a diamond ruff, draw the outstanding trumps, and lead a club to establish your twelfth trick in that suit.

Let's take a second look at that same heart holding. This time, though, dummy's trumps are not quite so good. Cover the E/W cards and see if you can see how to bring home your game:

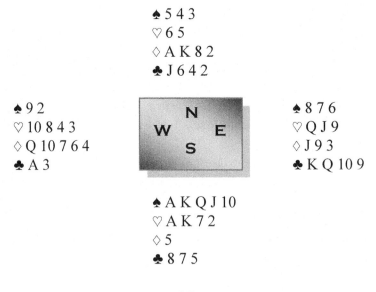

```
              ♠ 5 4 3
              ♡ 6 5
              ◊ A K 8 2
              ♣ J 6 4 2

♠ 9 2              N              ♠ 8 7 6
♡ 10 8 4 3    W       E          ♡ Q J 9
◊ Q 10 7 6 4      S              ◊ J 9 3
♣ A 3                            ♣ K Q 10 9

              ♠ A K Q J 10
              ♡ A K 7 2
              ◊ 5
              ♣ 8 7 5
```

Against your Four Spade contract, West leads the ♣A and continues the suit. East wins the second trick with the ♣10, cashes the ♣K (West throwing a heart) and continues with the ♣Q. You ruff the fourth round of clubs as West discards a second heart.

How should you play?

The defenders have already scored three tricks, so you must make the last ten. Five trumps in your hand and the two red-suit ace-kings add up to nine, but where can you find your tenth trick?

You have two losing hearts and one can be thrown on dummy's second diamond winner. Your only chance for an extra trick, though, appears to be via a heart ruff. However, there is a problem.

At the outset, there was a reasonable chance that you could safely ruff a heart in dummy. Now, with West having discarded two hearts already, one of the defenders is guaranteed to have at most only two hearts left, meaning that they will be able to ruff the third round of hearts with a trump bigger than any of those babies in the dummy.

Can you see how you might still be able to score a heart ruff in dummy?

With five hearts still outstanding, one of the defenders is certain to hold at least three cards in that suit. You must hope that same defender also holds at least three of the five missing trumps.

Let's see how the play might go: ruff the fourth round of clubs and cash two high trumps. Leaving both dummy and the defense each with one trump, you now cash dummy's diamond winners, discarding one of your low hearts. Now cash the ace and king of hearts and play the losing heart. You ruff in dummy whilst East, who holds the missing trump, must impotently follow suit. The only cards left in your hand now are winning trumps. Ten tricks – contract made.

Our next deal has some similarities to the previous one, but you will need to be careful if you are going to bring home your slam contract. Cover the E/W cards and see if you would manage to avoid the pitfalls:

```
              ♠ 7 6 3
              ♡ 8 5
              ◇ A Q 7 2
              ♣ K 7 5 2

♠ 9 2                                        ♠ 8 5 4
♡ Q 10            N                           ♡ K J 9 6 3
◇ J 10 8 4 3   W     E                        ◇ 9 6
♣ Q 10 8 3         S                          ♣ J 9 6

              ♠ A K Q J 10
              ♡ A 7 4 2
              ◇ K 5
              ♣ A 4
```

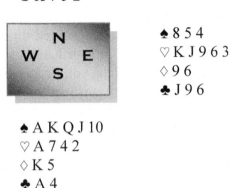

You reach Six Spades after an uncontested auction and West leads the ♠2. How do you play?

When you look for losers, you can find only three – the low hearts in your hand. One of these can be discarded on the third high diamond. One of the others, you will need to ruff in dummy. Can you see what might go wrong, though?

No one has been able to discard any hearts this time, but there is still a danger than one or other defender began with only a doubleton heart and will be able to ruff the third round higher than dummy.

Suppose you win the opening trump lead and immediately play the ♡A and a second round of hearts. West follows with the queen but East overtakes with the ♡K and plays a third round of hearts. You are about to ruff this trick in dummy when West rudely ruffs with the ♠9 in front of dummy's lower trumps. Well, that's a blow!

As we saw on the previous deal, you can still score a ruff in dummy when hearts split 5-2 as long as the defender with the doubleton heart holds no more than two trumps? You need, though, to play exactly two rounds of trumps before trying to take your heart ruff.

Suppose, then, that you win the opening trump lead and cash a second high trump before playing the ♡A and a second heart. East again overtakes his partner's queen of hearts with the king, but this time he spoils your plan by playing a third round of trumps. With no trump left in dummy, you can no longer score a ruff. You will be left with a losing heart at the end and again the contract will fail.

Hmmm! That didn't work either. If we play only one round of trumps, East plays a third heart and West scores a ruff. If we play two rounds of trumps, East plays a third round, denuding dummy. So, just how do we manage to score this heart ruff?

The answer is to force the defenders to make their decision before you make yours: win the opening lead and play a low heart from your hand. Whichever defender wins this trick does not matter – they can play neither a third round of hearts nor a third round of trumps.

Suppose the defenders switch to diamonds. You win with the ◇K, draw a second round of trumps and cash the ♡A. Now, when you play a third round of hearts, you will safely score your ruff in dummy if either the hearts split 4-3 or the defender with only two hearts also started with only two trumps.

Having taken your heart ruff, you cross back to the ♣A and draw the outstanding trump. You can then discard your fourth heart on dummy's diamonds and claim your contract. Slam bid and made!

Out next deal is an every-day game contract, but pay particular attention to the club suit. Let's see how the play might go:

♠ A 7 6 3 2
♡ 9 4
◇ Q 9 3 2
♣ Q 2

♠ K Q 10 9	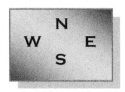	♠ J 8
♡ 10 6		♡ 8 5 2
◇ 8 4		◇ A J 10 7 6
♣ A 10 9 6 3		♣ J 8 4

♠ 5 4
♡ A K Q J 7 2
◇ K 5
♣ K 7 5

West attacks with the ♠K against your contract of Four Hearts.

How should you play?

You are now used to asking "If I draw trumps, will I have enough tricks for my contract?" Let's count them — six trumps in your hand and dummy's ace of spades gives your seven top tricks. You can also be fairly sure of making one trick by force in each minor suit, bringing your total to nine. It would still seem, though, that drawing trumps will leave you one trick short of your target, so an alternative strategy is needed.

The club suit on this deal is a combination that should alert you to the possibility of scoring a ruff in the short trump hand, and here that one extra trick will bump your total to the required ten.

So, how should we play?

Win the opening spade lead and immediately lead the queen of clubs. West wins with the ♣A, cashes the ♠Q and then plays a trump. You can now win in hand, cash the ♣K, and ruff the third round of clubs with dummy's last trump.

Having scored your ruff in dummy, you now want to draw the defenders' trumps as quickly as possible, so ruff a spade to get back to your hand and draw the outstanding trumps.

Only having finished drawing trumps is it now safe to set about establishing your winner in the diamond suit. You will eventually make six trumps in hand, your three side suit winners, and one ruff in dummy – ten tricks and contract made.

An initial trump lead would have defeated this contract, so it is lucky that West was dealt that attractive spade combination. I hope you quickly ruled out any notion of ducking the ace of spades at trick one — doing so would have given West a second chance to get a killing round of trumps in before you had knocked out the ♣A to set up your ruff.

The club suit on the next deal looks familiar, so perhaps the solution is the same:

                    ♠ A J 2
                    ♡ 9 8 2
                    ◇ Q 10 7 4 3
                    ♣ Q 4

♠ K Q 10 3   ♠ 9 8 7 5 4
♡ Q 10 4    ♡ J 6
◇ A 9 5   ◇ 8
♣ J 9 7   ♣ A 6 5 3 2

                    ♠ 6
                    ♡ A K 7 5 3
                    ◇ K J 6 2
                    ♣ K 10 8

West again leads the ♠K against your heart game.

How should you play?

Here is that same club holding that enables you to take an easy ruff
in the short trump hand. This time, because dummy has three trumps
rather than just two, perhaps you decide to play things safe by cashing
one high trump before starting on the clubs. So, win trick one with the
♠A, play a trump to the ace, and then lead a club to dummy's queen.
You will be able to win the trump return or ruff the spade
continuation, take your club ruff, then draw trumps and knock out the
ace of diamonds.

"Oh. What's this though?"

When East wins trick three with the ace of clubs he switches to the
eight of diamonds. West wins with the ◇A and plays a second round of
the suit, ruffed by East with the ♡J. East only now plays a second
spade, which you ruff. West still has the guarded ♡Q, so you will have
to lose a fourth trick and you are one down.

That was jolly unlucky!

Or, was it?

Just as a side suit such as these clubs should alert you to the
possibility of scoring an extra trick via a ruff, so should the diamond
holding here warn you of the danger of a defensive ruff. Remember
that when (as declarer) you ruff one of your losers, you are effectively

ruffing one of the defenders' winners. What's good for the goose, though, is equally good for the gander, and the rotten opponents will be only too happy to try to ruff your winners if you give them the chance.

Playing for a club ruff on this deal means that declarer has forgotten to ask what should by now be a familiar question. Counting tricks, you can see that there are ten tricks available simply by drawing trumps (four in each red suit and one in each black suit) — it is, therefore, time to draw trumps..

With two side-suit aces to lose, a bad trump split is likely to scupper the contract anyway, so declarer should play on the assumption that they will split 3-2. So, win the ♠A at trick one and immediately cash the two top trumps. Once both defenders follow suit, you are just about home.

What makes this deal so different from the previous one?

This time, you have a source of tricks in a side suit. This means that there is no rush to dispose of the third-round club loser: you can see that there will be a discard available on the fifth round of diamonds once the defenders' trumps have been removed.

Of course, you should always be aware of the opportunity to score extra tricks by ruffing in the short trump hand. Having spotted that possibility, though, do not let it obscure your view of the complete deal. There may be alternative and less dangerous routes to the required number of tricks.

The presence of a strong side suit in either your hand or in dummy is often a good indicator that you should draw trumps as quickly as possible. Do not give the defenders a chance to ruff your winners if you can see enough tricks to fulfill your contract.

Take a look at our next deal: cover the E/W cards and decide how you would play Four Spades on the lead of the ♡10:

Both Vul: Dealer South

♠ J 10 4
♡ 8 7 6 5
♢ 8 5
♣ A K 6 3

♠ 9 7 5
♡ 10 9
♢ A Q 10 4 3
♣ 10 8 4

N
W E
S

♠ 8 3
♡ Q J 4 2
♢ 9 6 2
♣ Q J 9 5

♠ A K Q 6 2
♡ A K 3
♢ K J 7
♣ 7 2

West	North	East	South
—	—	—	1♠
Pass	2♠	Pass	4♠
All Pass			

By now, you know the general rule is that you should draw trumps immediately unless there is a good reason not to do so. These are the main reasons why you might choose to delay drawing trumps:

* You need to take one or more ruffs in the short-trump hand
* You need to take a quick discard
* You must set up a discard
* You will need dummy's trumps as entries to establish a suit and/or enjoy late winners

Do any of those apply on this deal? Count your losers – potentially one in hearts and three in diamonds. That's one too many. How might you be able to avoid one of those losers?

The odds are excellent that East will hold one of the missing diamond honors, so perhaps you can simply draw trumps, cross to dummy in clubs, and lead a diamond towards your hand. Your ♢J loses to West's queen but you can still win the club return and lead a second diamond from dummy. When your ◇K also loses, though, you are one down. That was unlucky, or was it?

Go back to the list above and ask yourself whether you could have taken any of those steps before drawing trumps.

Let me ask a slightly different question: how would have played this hand if you had held three low diamonds in your hand rather than K-J-x? Would you not have won the heart lead and immediately played a diamond from hand?

Whatever the defenders do, they cannot then stop you from ruffing the third round of diamonds in dummy. It is easy to allow the diamond honors to blind you to the right line of play here. Play any diamond from hand at trick two and you are a tempo ahead.

Note that a trump lead would have defeated this contract legitimately (assuming West plays trumps every time he gets in). If you play even a single round of trumps before leading diamonds, you give the initiative back to West.

We have so far seen the two primary methods of creating tricks in addition to your top winners – taking ruffs in the short trump hand and establishing long tricks in a side suit. On the next deal, you can combine these two methods in search of an overtrick, but your primary aim is still to guarantee making your contract.

```
              ♠ A 8 2
              ♡ Q 9 7 5 2
              ◇ 9 6 4 3
              ♣ 6

  ♠ 6 5 4          N          ♠ 7
  ♡ A J 3      W       E      ♡ K 10 8 6 4
  ◇ J 10 5         S          ◇ K Q
  ♣ K Q J 5                   ♣ 10 9 7 4 3

              ♠ K Q J 10 9 3
              ♡ —
              ◇ A 8 7 2
              ♣ A 8 2
```

West leads the ♣K against your Four Spade contract. How should you play to make the maximum number of tricks whilst ensuring at least ten?

Start by counting your tricks: six trumps in hand plus two minor-suit aces bring your total to eight. You may be able to develop a long diamond trick if the defenders' diamonds split (although this is hardly guaranteed). Even so, that adds only one trick, and you are two short of your target, so you clearly cannot afford to draw trumps immediately.

Fortunately, your bow has another string: ruffing both of your losing clubs in dummy will supplement your top winners by two, bringing the number of sure tricks up to ten without relying on any suit to behave.

This, then, should be your primary objective. Win the opening club lead and ruff a club with the ♠8. Now cross back to your hand by playing dummy's remaining low trump to an honor in hand (noting that both defenders follow suit), and ruff your last club with dummy's ♠A. You can now ruff a heart with a high trump and draw the rest of the defenders' trumps.

Your contract assured, you can now try to set up a long diamond winner for an overtrick. Cash the ◇A and continue with a second round of that suit. When both defenders follow, you know the suit is breaking. Ruff the heart or club return and play a third round of diamonds. You can take the rest of the tricks now with your trumps and the long diamond.

Notice how we used a round of trumps to get back to hand after ruffing the first club. We could have ruffed a heart, but we only needed to ruff two clubs in dummy, so we could afford one round of trumps. Taking a ruff first, drawing one round of trumps, and then taking the second ruff with the ace of trumps, ensured that there was no chance of anything nasty happening.

Notice too, that if we had ruffed a club, ruffed a heart back to hand, ruffed the second club low and then cashed the ♠A, we would then be stranded in dummy with trumps still outstanding. Getting back to hand via a second heart ruff would mean that we eventually run out of trumps before we are able to establish the long diamond. Getting back to hand by playing a diamond to the ace would work most of the time, but we would be rather sick if today was the day that West was dealt no diamonds, and ruffed our ace, wouldn't we?

Don't tempt fate if it is possible to avoid doing so. The Bridge Gods are apt to punish one for taking liberties with their largesse.

On the previous deal, we combined 'ruffing losers' and 'setting up long tricks'. On the next deal, we again have a club loser to ruff and a diamond suit to establish, so is the situation the same? Cover the E/W cards if you want to decide for yourself before reading on:

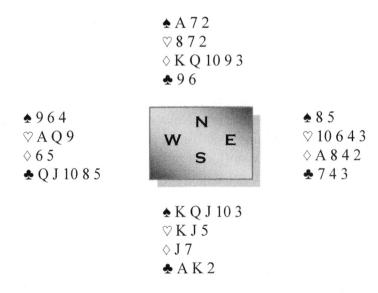

♠ A 7 2
♡ 8 7 2
◇ K Q 10 9 3
♣ 9 6

♠ 9 6 4
♡ A Q 9
◇ 6 5
♣ Q J 10 8 5

♠ 8 5
♡ 10 6 4 3
◇ A 8 4 2
♣ 7 4 3

♠ K Q J 10 3
♡ K J 5
◇ J 7
♣ A K 2

You bid to Four Spades uncontested and West leads the ♣Q. How should you continue?

We've seen this situation before, haven't we? We should win the opening lead, cash the second club winner and ruff our club loser. We can then draw trumps and set about the diamonds.

Oh dear! The mean opponents do not take their ace of diamonds until the second round. Then East wins and plays a heart through your honors. You try the jack, but West wins with the queen and exits safely with a fourth round of clubs, which you have to ruff.

With no entry to dummy's diamond winners you are now forced to lead a heart away from the king at the end, and the defenders score two more winners in the suit. You are one down, having lost three hearts and one diamond.

Actually, just about all you need to make this contract is a 3-2 trump break. If you stop to count your tricks, you will see that you potentially have five spades, four diamonds and two clubs. What appears to be an extra trick provided by the club ruff is actually an illusion. What is vital on this deal is that you establish the diamonds AND reach them after trumps have been drawn. However, the only certain entry to dummy is the ace of trumps.

Having recognized this, the play is straightforward: win the club lead and immediately cash two high trumps from your hand. When both defenders follow suit, leave the last trump outstanding and set about the diamonds, leading the jack from your hand. If the jack holds, persist with a second diamond, forcing the defenders to take their ace.

Suppose West wins and plays a second round of clubs. You can win, cross to dummy with the ♠A (drawing the last trump at the same time) and cash three diamond winners, discarding losers. The defenders will make just one more trick at the end — eleven tricks.

(If East either switches to a heart or plays a third diamond when he wins the ◊A, the defense will hold you to ten tricks, but they can never threaten your contract.)

Now you've got the idea of projecting the play before committing yourself, try your hand at the next deal by covering the E/W cards.

```
                    ♠ 4
                    ♡ K 9 7 5
                    ◊ 9 8 6 5 2
                    ♣ A K 6

  ♠ K J 9 8 5 2          N              ♠ 10 7 3
  ♡ J 8 2         W             E       ♡ Q 4
  ◊ A J 3                 S             ◊ 7 4
  ♣ 9                                   ♣ Q 10 8 5 4 3

                    ♠ A Q 6
                    ♡ A 10 6 3
                    ◊ K Q 10
                    ♣ J 7 2
```

You open with a strong notrump and West overcalls in spades. Partner makes a takeout double and your duly reach game in your 4-4 heart fit. How should you play on the lead of the ♣9?

Counting tells you that even if trumps break 3-2 you have four possible losers – one heart, one club and two diamonds. You also need to do something with your two losing spades, so plenty of work to be done yet..

Faced with this deal, most declarers would look no further than taking spade ruffs and drawing trumps as the first priority. Let's see what happens if we set about playing the hand in that manner: you win the club lead in dummy, play a spade to the ace and ruff a spade. You can now play two high trumps ending in hand and ruff your last spade. When you then play a diamond to the king, though, West wins, cashes his trump winner, and forces your last trump with a fourth round of spades. In due course, West will get in with the ◊J and cash his remaining spade winners to beat your contract by a trick or two.

Disappointing as this outcome may be, is this a particularly surprising turn of events?

By playing the deal through in your head before actually playing any cards, you can foresee this possibility. There are two clues to the right line of play – West's overcall suggests that he is likely, although not certain, to hold the ◊A. More significantly, though, his opening lead almost guarantees that he began with at most two clubs. Can you see how to take advantage of this information?

One reasonable line of play is to win the opening club lead in dummy and immediately play a diamond to the king. If West wins and plays a second club, you will win with dummy's second honor, cash two high trumps ending in dummy, and then play a diamond to your ten.

Even if West can win this trick and cash a trump, he can do you no damage as he has no more clubs. The best he can do is to exit with his third diamond, but you can then ruff a spade with dummy's last trump and, in doing so, reach dummy's two winning diamonds on which you will discard your remaining black-suit losers.

(If the ◊K wins at trick two, you will cash your two high trumps ending in dummy and lead a second diamond to the queen to reach a similar position.)

On the two previous deals, your first inclination was probably to try ruffing losers in dummy. By projecting how the play was likely to go if you followed that route, though, you were able to see that it would not work. In both instances, the winning option was to set up dummy's weak side suit and use a late ruff as an entry to the established winners.

You must have noticed how expert players often seem able to sidestep the effect of bad breaks. Our final deal in this chapter looks very simple and, for that reason, is just the sort of hand on which many players would come unstuck.

Cover the E/W cards and decide how you would play before reading on:

Both Vul: Dealer South

```
                    ♠ J 10 5 4
                    ♡ 7 5
                    ◇ 8 6
                    ♣ A 10 8 6 3

  ♠ —                    N           ♠ 8 7 3
  ♡ K 9 8 2         W         E      ♡ Q J 4
  ◇ K J 4 3              S           ◇ A 9 7 2
  ♣ K Q J 7 5                        ♣ 9 4 2

                    ♠ A K Q 9 6 2
                    ♡ A 10 6 3
                    ◇ Q 10 5
                    ♣ —
```

West	North	East	South
—	—	—	1♠
Dble	3♠	Pass	4♠
All Pass			

You bid to Four Spades after a takeout double by West and a pre-emptive raise by your partner. West kicks off with the ♣K.

How do you play?

41

It looks natural to win with the ♣A and discard a heart loser at trick one. I suspect that many players faced with this deal would then immediately play a trump at trick two.

If that was your first inclination, remember to **ALWAYS** stop and count before doing anything. Counting losers from the point of view of declarer's hand, you can see six – three in each red suit. One of these can be thrown on the ♣A, but how are you going to get rid of two more? The answer is that you can ruff them in dummy, but you can only take two ruffs if you have two trumps left to do so.

Let's see what happens if you discard a heart on the ♣A at trick one and then play a round of trumps. Whatever you do next, East cannot be prevented from gaining the lead twice, once in each red suit, and each time he is in he will play a trump. When the time comes to ruff your last loser, dummy will be out of trumps.

A better approach is to discard a diamond on the ♣A and then to immediately lead a heart to the ace and exit with a second heart. The defenders can play a trump now, but you will win in hand, ruff one heart loser, cross back to hand with a second round of trumps, and ruff your last heart. It is now a simple matter of ruffing a club and drawing East's last trump before claiming your contract, conceding two diamonds to the defense.

Of course, if trumps split 2-1, everyone and their dog would make the same ten tricks on this deal. When trumps divide 3-0, though, as they will rather more often than you might expect, only those who project how the play might go will manage to bring home their contract. By now, I hope you are one of those players.

Quiz Hands

1.

♠ J 7 6
♡ 8 5
♢ Q 9 6 2
♣ Q J 5 2

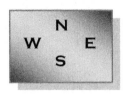

♠ A K Q 10 4
♡ A 7 2
♢ K 5
♣ K 7 4

West leads a trump against Four Spades. How do you play?
(If you play on hearts, the defense leads a second trump.)

2.

♠ J 4
♡ 7 5 2
♢ A J 8 5 4
♣ J 6 3

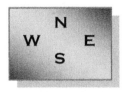

♠ A K 6 2
♡ A K 9 6 3
♢ 7
♣ A 7 2

You reach Four Hearts in an unopposed auction. West leads the ♠10 and East covers dummy's jack with the queen. How do you play?

3.

♠ A 6 5 3
♡ Q 8 6 5
◇ 6 4
♣ Q 8 2

♠ 8 4
♡ 3
◇ A K 5 3
♣ A K J 9 5 3

West leads the ♠Q against your Five Club contract. How do you play?

4.

♠ 10 6 3
♡ A 9 8 5
◇ 6
♣ A J 6 5 2

♠ A K 8 5 4
♡ 7
◇ A K J 8 5 3
♣ 7

West leads the ♡K against your Six Spade contract. How do you play?

Answers to Quiz Hands

1.

♠ J 7 6
♡ 8 5
◇ Q 9 6 2
♣ Q J 5 2

♠ 9 3
♡ J 10 6 3
◇ A 8 4
♣ A 10 9 3

N
W E
S

♠ 8 5 2
♡ K Q 9 4
◇ J 10 7 3
♣ 8 6

♠ A K Q 10 4
♡ A 7 2
◇ K 5
♣ K 7 4

You reach Four Spades against which West leads a trump.

Let's count losers – two in hearts and one in each minor. You cannot do anything about the missing aces, so you will need to avoid losing one of the small hearts. Fortunately, dummy has only two hearts, so you can take a ruff. Will that give us enough tricks? Five trumps in hand, the ♡A and a heart ruff is seven and we can establish two clubs and one diamond by force, bringing the total to ten.

Win the opening trump lead in hand with the ♠10, cash the ♡A and play a second heart, setting up the ruff in dummy. West wins the second round of hearts and perseveres with a second trump. Again, you win in hand and now you lead your third heart and ruff with the ♠J.

You now need to get back to your hand to draw the outstanding trump. Whichever minor you lead, if you find East with the ace, the defense cannot stop you getting to hand with the king. Suppose you decide to try a club. You play a club to your king but West wins and exits with a second round of clubs to dummy's queen. Okay, so let's try a diamond now. You lead a low diamond to your king and again West produces the ace. He now plays a third round of clubs and you put up dummy's jack, but East ruffs while you have to follow suit.

That nasty club ruff is the fourth defensive trick and your contract is one down.

What went wrong?

As a matter of general technique, when you are trying to get to your hand to draw an outstanding trump, you should try to do so using the suit in which your partnership holds the fewest cards, since that then reduces the risk that the defenders can score a ruff,. Had you instead tried a diamond to the king after taking your heart ruff, your king would still have lost to West's ace but you would eventually have made it to hand by ruffing the third round of diamonds. You could then have drawn the last trump before the defenders could set up a ruff of their own.

2.

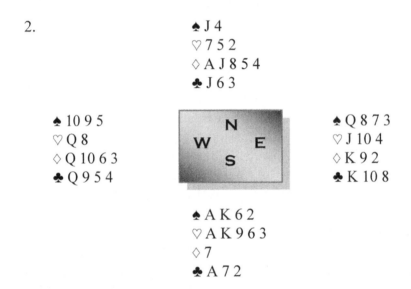

♠ J 4
♡ 7 5 2
♢ A J 8 5 4
♣ J 6 3

♠ 10 9 5
♡ Q 8
♢ Q 10 6 3
♣ Q 9 5 4

♠ Q 8 7 3
♡ J 10 4
♢ K 9 2
♣ K 10 8

♠ A K 6 2
♡ A K 9 6 3
♢ 7
♣ A 7 2

Against your Four Heart contact, the opening ten of spades lead is covered by the jack, queen and king.

You cannot avoid losing one trump (you hope it is only one!) and there are also two losers in each black suit. The only possible way to reduce this loser-count to three is by taking two ruffs in dummy. However, you cannot hope to ruff both of your small spades: on the fourth round of the suit one or other defender will surely produce a trump higher than dummy's seven. So, what can be done?

The solution is to ruff a club instead! Win the spade lead, cash the other top spade and ruff a spade. Now duck a club. It will not assist the defense for East to win and play a fourth round of spades — West can ruff with the ♡8 but you will discard a club from dummy. You will then subsequently ruff a club, losing just one club trick and two tricks in trumps.

If the defenders return something else when you duck a club, you will play a fourth round of spades yourself. Whichever defender holds the last spade, you will be able to discard a club from dummy and subsequently take a club ruff for your tenth trick.

3.

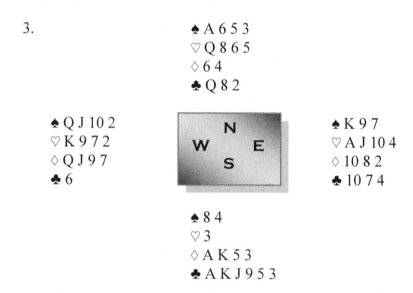

        ♠ A 6 5 3
        ♡ Q 8 6 5
        ◇ 6 4
        ♣ Q 8 2

♠ Q J 10 2   ♠ K 9 7
♡ K 9 7 2   ♡ A J 10 4
◇ Q J 9 7   ◇ 10 8 2
♣ 6   ♣ 10 7 4

        ♠ 8 4
        ♡ 3
        ◇ A K 5 3
        ♣ A K J 9 5 3

West leads the ♠Q against Five Clubs. A count reveals four losers, two diamonds and one in each major. There does not seem to be any way to avoid losing the tricks in the majors, so you will need to take two diamond ruffs to go along with your nine high-card winners.

Needing only two ruffs in dummy, perhaps you think you can afford to draw one round of trumps first, but entries to your hand are limited. Play it through and see what happens if you do draw a round of trumps – after taking your first diamond ruff you will not have a quick re-entry to your hand, and the opponents will be able to play a second round of trumps, leaving you will a diamond to lose at the end,

Having won the opening lead with the ♠A, you must immediately cash the ace-king of diamonds and lead a third diamond to ruff in dummy. (Ruffing with the eight reduces the chance of East being able to overruff, but you cannot afford to ruff this diamond higher.) Now is the time to play the first round of trumps, re-entering your hand in the process. The fourth round of diamonds can now be ruffed with dummy's last trump, the queen. You can now exit in a major and the defense will cash their two winners, but you only have trumps remaining now and you can claim the rest: eleven tricks and contract made.

4.

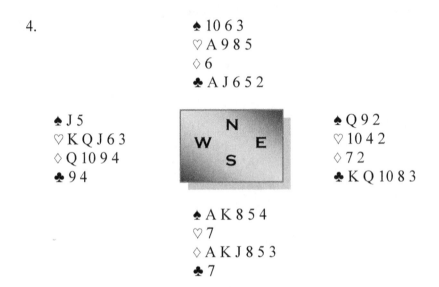

♠ 10 6 3
♡ A 9 8 5
◇ 6
♣ A J 6 5 2

♠ J 5
♡ K Q J 6 3
◇ Q 10 9 4
♣ 9 4

♠ Q 9 2
♡ 10 4 2
◇ 7 2
♣ K Q 10 8 3

♠ A K 8 5 4
♡ 7
◇ A K J 8 5 3
♣ 7

West leads the ♡K against your spade slam.

You will need the trumps to break 3-2. Even then, though, barring an unlikely queen-jack doubleton, you will still have to lose one trump trick. You will, therefore, need to make all of the remaining tricks if you are to bring home your rather ambitious slam contract.

Clearly, you will need to score some diamond tricks. One option is to draw two rounds of trumps immediately with your ace and king, and then to play diamonds, ruffing the third round. If the opponents' diamonds divide 3-3 or if the queen falls doubleton, you will now be able to claim your contract. Can you see how you might improve on those odds?

You can still prevail even if one of the defenders holds four diamonds headed by the queen as long as the defender with the doubleton diamond also has the three-card trump holding.

Let's see how the play might go: win the ♡A at trick one, immediately play a diamond to your ace and ruff a diamond. If the queen appears, your problems in that suit are over, so let's assume that it does not. You can now cross back to hand with a round of trumps and lead another low diamond. When West follows suit, you ruff with dummy's last trump. If the diamonds were 3-3 all along, East will follow and you can take a ruff back to hand, cash your second high spade and, if both defenders follow suit, claim your contract losing just one trump trick.

This line of play also succeeds if East has no more diamonds provided that he also started with the three card trump holding (as in the diagram). He can overruff the third round of diamonds, but he is doing so with the defenders' natural trump trick. You will eventually get back to hand, cash your second high spade, dropping the defenders' two remaining cards in the suit, and the king of diamonds will now bring down the queen.

Note that you will fail if you make the mistake of cashing both the ace and king of diamonds before taking your first ruff. East will be able to overruff the third round of diamonds and, when you then take your second diamond ruff, he will again be able to overruff dummy.

Chapter 3 – Establishing Discards Before Drawing Trumps

We have already seen that you should draw trumps as quickly as possible if you can see enough tricks to make your contract. We have also identified some reasons why you might delay drawing trumps:

* You need to take ruffs in the short-trump hand;
* You will need dummy's trumps as late entries;
* You need to take a quick discard;
* You must set up a discard.

In the previous chapter, we looked at some deals on which you needed to take ruffs in the short trump hand. We now turn our attention to hands on which discards are crucial. Here is a straightforward example:

♠ Q 9 2
♡ A K 4
◇ Q 9 5 4
♣ J 9 4

♠ 8 5		♠ A 5
♡ Q J 9 6		♡ 10 5 2
◇ A 10 7 3		◇ J 8 6 2
♣ 10 6 2		♣ A 8 7 3

♠ K J 10 7 4 3
♡ 8 7 3
◇ K
♣ K Q 5

You reach Four Spades and West leads kicks off the defense with the ♡Q. How do you play?

Playing in no-trumps, the normal method of planning the play is to start by counting your tricks. In a suit contract, though, your primary assessment is done by counting losers (and only then counting tricks to make sure that there are enough). This deal illustrates why this is so: if you simply count your winners, you are likely to come to the conclusion that you have five trumps and two top hearts, and that you can establish three more tricks in the minors (one diamond and two clubs) by force. With the number of winners apparently adding up to ten, might you not then decide that you should start drawing trumps immediately?

Let us instead count losers: in addition to the three missing aces you also have a potential heart loser – four in total.

Wait a moment. This doesn't seem to add up: there are four losers but ten winners? The reason for this apparent discrepancy is that by the time you set up and cash all of those minor-suit winners, you will have only trumps left in your hand. Two of your winners will, therefore, fall on the same trick.

On this deal, you can do nothing to stop the defenders taking their aces, so you will need to dispose of the heart loser if you are going to fulfill your contract. Where can that loser go?

The obvious place is on dummy's queen of diamonds, so you will need to promote that card to master status before the defenders can cash a heart trick.

If you play a trump at trick two, the defenders will take their ace and lead a second round of hearts, removing your second stopper in the suit. When they then get in with one of their minor-suit aces they will have enough cashing winners to defeat your contract.

Instead, win the opening heart lead in dummy and immediately play the king of diamonds. West captures your king with his ace and leads a second heart, but you can now win in dummy and cash the queen of diamonds in order to discard the losing heart from your hand.

Having reduced your losers to an acceptable number you are now ready to set about drawing trumps.

As beginners, we all learned how it was possible to make extra tricks (in addition to just our high cards) by taking a finesse. As players improve, they learn the rather more difficult lesson of when NOT to take a finesse.

Our next deal offers you a straight 50-50 chance of making your contract, but wouldn't you rather enjoy better odds than that?

Cover the E/W cards and decide whether this is a deal on which you should start drawing trumps immediately:

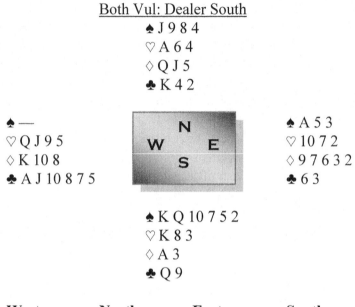

Both Vul: Dealer South

♠ J 9 8 4
♡ A 6 4
◊ Q J 5
♣ K 4 2

♠ —
♡ Q J 9 5
◊ K 10 8
♣ A J 10 8 7 5

♠ A 5 3
♡ 10 7 2
◊ 9 7 6 3 2
♣ 6 3

♠ K Q 10 7 5 2
♡ K 8 3
◊ A 3
♣ Q 9

West	North	East	South
—	—	—	1♠
2♣	3♣	Pass	4♠
All Pass			

West overcalls your One Spade opening and your partner cue-bids to show at least an invitational raise of your suit. Your jump to game concludes a brief auction.

West leads the ♡Q. What is your plan?

A quick count of your losers reveals that there may be one too many: two black aces, one heart and possibly one diamond. If East holds the ◊K then you can avoid losing a trick in that suit by taking a successful finesse, but are you happy to settle for an even-money chance?

There is a much better option available – to establish a diamond winner in dummy on which you can dispose of your heart loser. Time, though, is of the essence: if you win the opening lead and immediately set about driving out the ace of trumps, the defenders will continue hearts. They will then have established their heart winner before you have anywhere to throw your loser.

You must set up your discard right away.

Be careful, though: suppose you win the opening heart lead in dummy with the ace in order to run the $\diamond$Q.

West wins with the king and leads a second heart. You can win with the $\heartsuit$K and cash the $\diamond$A: you now have a winning diamond in dummy but no way to reach it without letting the opponents gain the lead. Whichever black suit you play next, the defenders will take their ace and cash their heart trick to defeat your game.

You must, instead, win the opening heart lead in your hand with the king and immediately cash the $\diamond$A and lead a second diamond, forcing out the king. Note that you do not care which defender holds the missing king.

When you then win the heart continuation with the ace you are conveniently in dummy to cash the $\diamond$Q and throw the heart loser from your hand. Having taken care of urgent business, you can now drive out the ace of trumps.

Note that if dummy's diamonds had been only Q-x-x (rather than Q-J-x), the best line of play would have been the same. Of course, you would then need to find West with the $\diamond$K, but at least you would have a 50% chance whereas any alternative line of play has virtually no chance of success.

On our next deal, you do not need to set up a discard. Should you, therefore, set about drawing trumps immediately?

N/S Game: Dealer West

♠ A Q 7 3
♡ K Q 5 2
◇ 8 3
♣ A 5 2

♠ 10 8 2
♡ 8
◇ K Q 10 9 7 6
♣ Q 10 7

♠ J 9 6 4
♡ A 6 4
◇ J 4 2
♣ K J 3

♠ K 5
♡ J 10 9 7 3
◇ A 5
♣ 9 8 6 4

West	North	East	South
2◇	Dble	Pass	3♡
Pass	4♡	All Pass	

West opens a weak two bid in diamonds. Your partner doubles for takeout and raises your encouraging jump response to game. West now leads the ◇K against your heart game. How should you play?

You appear to have enough tricks for your contract. However, the diamond lead has established a winner for the defense in that suit so there is a danger of losing four tricks before you can cash ten winners.

If you win the opening diamond lead and immediately force out the ace of trumps, the defenders will cash their diamond trick. Unless one defender (presumably East here) holds at least four cards in each black suit, permitting you to squeeze him, you will eventually lose two club tricks and your contract will be one down.

As a general principle, when you play in a suit contract you would avoid cashing your winners until trumps have been drawn. After all, the defenders are also allowed to score tricks with their trumps if you let them. Of course, though, there are exceptions to every rule, and sometimes the conservative approach is not an option.

Here you have a discard available on the third round of spades, but using that discard to dispose of the fourth club from your hand will not help. (The fourth club is not a loser since it can be ruffed in dummy.) You need to dispose of the diamond loser before allowing the defense to gain the lead: after winning the ◊A at trick one, cash your three spade winners discarding the low diamond from your hand.

Of course, sometimes the third (or even the second) round of spades will get ruffed. If so, that's just too bad as you were then unlikely to make the contract whatever you tried. Giving yourself a chance must surely be better than resigning yourself to defeat by taking a line of play that you can see is certain to fail, isn't it?

Sometimes you have a discard available but no obvious loser to throw on it. Listening carefully to the bidding on the next deal provides the clue you need to bring home your contact. Even so, you will need to think somewhat 'outside the box': cover the E/W cards and see if you can spot the winning line of play.

<u>N/S Game: Dealer East</u>

♠ K 10 5 3
♡ K 7 6 2
◊ A K
♣ K 6 2

♠ 6   ♠ A 4
♡ 10 8 4 3   ♡ A J 9
◊ J 10 9 6   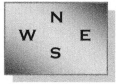   ◊ Q 8 7 4 3 2
♣ Q 9 8 3   ♣ J 10

♠ Q J 9 8 7 2
♡ Q 5
◊ 5
♣ A 7 5 4

West	North	East	South
—	—	1◊	1♠
3◊	4♠	5◊	Pass
Pass	5♠	All Pass	

You reach Four Spades but the non-vulnerable opponents sacrifice. Your partner soldiers on to the 5-level in search of the vulnerable game bonus and West leads the ◊J.

Can you justify partner's optimism?

You seem to have three losers, two aces and the third round of clubs. The fourth club can be ruffed in dummy after drawing trumps and you can set up your heart winner any time, so is there a reason to delay drawing trumps?

With no obvious way to avoid any of the losers, most players would play a trump at trick two more in the vague hope that "something good will happen" than with any particular plan in mind.

East takes his ace of trumps immediately and plays a second round of diamonds. "That king of diamonds is worthless – why couldn't he have held something useful like the queen of clubs?"

Is the ◊K really of no value, though?

Could you not throw one of your losers on it?

The bidding has revealed the location of the opponents' high cards: East's opening bid virtually marks him with both major-suit aces. Can you see how this knowledge helps?

Let's see what happens if, instead of leading a trump at trick two, you lead a low heart from dummy: what can East do?

Suppose, first, that East plays low, allowing your ♡Q to win. Re-entering dummy with the ♣K to cash that 'useless' king of diamonds, you can now dispose of your second heart and draw trumps. Ruffing your fourth club in dummy, you will now lose just one club and the trump ace – eleven tricks.

Suppose, instead, that East rises with his ace of hearts at trick two. He plays a second diamond, but this time you discard a club as dummy's ◊K wins. Now you can force out the ace of trumps, unblock the ♡Q and, eventually, discard your remaining club loser on dummy's ♡K. Once again, contract made.

Partner's king of diamonds wasn't so useless after all, was it?

You have a fast discard available on our next deal, too. Should you make use of the early opportunity to dispose of a loser, though?

N/S Game: Dealer West

 ♠ A 8 6 4
 ♡ K 2
 ◇ 8 5 3
 ♣ A K 7 4

♠ Q 7 3   ♠ K J 10 9 5 2
♡ Q 10 9 8 5 4   N   ♡ J 6
◇ K 9 4   W   E   ◇ 7
♣ J   S   ♣ Q 10 9 3

 ♠ —
 ♡ A 7 3
 ◇ A Q J 10 6 2
 ♣ 8 6 5 2

West	North	East	South
2♡	Dble	2♠	3♡
3♠	Pass	Pass	5◇
All Pass			

West leads the ♠3 against your 5-level game. How do you play?

You have three potential losers outside the trump suit. Remembering West's opening weak two bid in hearts, you realize that East will hold at most two cards in that suit

Unless trumps break 2-2, it seems that you will not be able to ruff your heart loser in dummy without East overruffing. You want the lead in dummy to take the trump finesse, so perhaps you decide to win the opening lead with dummy's ♠A and discard your third heart?

You may indeed use dummy's ace of spades to deal with your third heart, but is there any rush to do so?

Suppose, instead, that you play low from dummy and ruff the opening lead in your hand. You can then cross to dummy with the ♡K to take the trump finesse. West wins with the ◇K and returns a second spade, which you again win by ruffing. When you now draw a second round of trumps, East discards, meaning that you can safely cash the ♡A and ruff your losing heart in dummy. Returning to hand by ruffing

57

dummy's remaining low spade, you draw West's last trump.

The ♠A remains in dummy to take care of one of your low clubs, meaning that you no longer care how that suit splits. The defenders' clubs turn out to be 4-1, so it would have been fatal to use the discard on dummy's ace of spades to dispose of a heart. If there is no pressing need for a fast discard, it will often be right to delay taking a winner until you are sure which loser to throw.

Sometimes the decision 'when to draw trumps' is somewhat ethereal. Cover the E/W cards and see how you fare on the next deal:

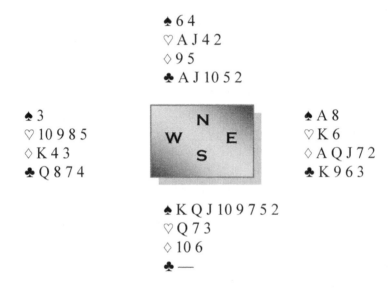

```
              ♠ 6 4
              ♡ A J 4 2
              ◇ 9 5
              ♣ A J 10 5 2

♠ 3                          ♠ A 8
♡ 10 9 8 5         N         ♡ K 6
◇ K 4 3        W     E       ◇ A Q J 7 2
♣ Q 8 7 4          S         ♣ K 9 6 3

              ♠ K Q J 10 9 7 5 2
              ♡ Q 7 3
              ◇ 10 6
              ♣ —
```

With neither side vulnerable, you open Four Spades and East's double closes the auction. West leads the ♡10. How should you play?

Both the bidding and the opening lead suggest that the ♡K is offside, so winning with the ♡A in order to pitch a diamond loser on dummy's ace of clubs looks clear. Is it now time to play trumps?

Doing so gives the defense a chance: East wins the ♠A and cashes the ♡K. He can see that just cashing a top diamond is likely to concede ten tricks (and -590 will be bad even at matchpoints). East's only chance is to find his partner with the ◇K, so he underleads his ace, putting West on lead to deliver a heart ruff to defeat the contract.

That was unlucky. Or was it? How might you have avoided this?

You need to disrupt the defenders' communications. This can be done in one of two ways: at trick three, rather than a trump, note the effect of playing a diamond (or a club and discarding the last diamond from your hand). Although West gains the lead, he does so at a time when the hearts are still blocked, preventing the killing ruff.

Anticipating problems before they occur can enable you to sidestep them. When dummy first appears on the next deal, you might wish you had bid a slam. If would be a shame, therefore, to go down in game

Both Game: Dealer East

```
                ♠ 7 5
                ♡ Q 6 4 3
                ◇ A Q 8
                ♣ K 10 7 3

♠ Q 10 9 8 4 2        N           ♠ A K J 6 3
♡ J 7 2          W         E      ♡ A 8 5
◇ 5                   S           ◇ 10 9 6 4 2
♣ Q J 5                           ♣ —

                ♠ —
                ♡ K 10 2
                ◇ K J 7 3
                ♣ A 9 8 6 4 2
```

West	North	East	South
—	—	1♠	2♣
4♠	5♣	All Pass	

West leads the ◇5 against Five Clubs. How do you play?

If you had bid to Six Clubs and found trumps breaking 2-1, the fate of your contract would have depended on finding a favorable heart position. Having stopped in game, you might think that the bad trump split means that you will now have to rely on the hearts to make eleven tricks.

When the deal occurred as the table, this is indeed what happened, but only because declarer was careless. Having won the opening diamond lead with dummy's ace, declarer then cashed the ♣K, revealing the bad break. Too late, he ruffed a spade, cashed the ♣A and tried to re-enter dummy with the ◇Q. West ruffed in with his trump trick and exited with a spade, leaving declarer at the mercy of the heart position. Quite rightly, the Bridge Gods did not see fit to forgive and the contract failed when declarer found himself with two hearts losers.

Faced with what looked like an apparently easy contract, declarer's fatal error was in failing to ask 'What can go wrong?' If you anticipate the 3-0 trump break, it is not difficult to see that you might need an endplay to guarantee eleven tricks. Note the difference if declarer takes the small precaution of ruffing a spade at trick two. He can then cash the top trumps and, using the ♣K as a second entry to dummy, ruff a second spade to eliminate that suit.

Now, it does not matter how the diamonds split. At some point, West will either ruff in with or be thrown in with his trump trick, and forced either to concede a ruff-and-sluff or to lead into declarer's heart tenace.

Quiz Hands

1.

       ♠ A J 10 3
       ♡ J 7 6 2
       ♢ K Q
       ♣ 8 7 3

       ♠ 6 2
       ♡ K Q 10 9 4 3
       ♢ 8 7
       ♣ A K 2

You open One Heart and are soon installed in game.
West leads the ♣J against Four Hearts. How do you play?

2.

       ♠ A 10
       ♡ A 5 2
       ♢ A 9 5 4 2
       ♣ 9 6 3

       ♠ K Q J 8 5 4
       ♡ 7 4 3
       ♢ 8
       ♣ A 7 2

You reach Four Spades in an uncontested auction.
West leads the ♢K. How do you play?

1.

♠ A J 10 3
♡ J 7 6 2
◇ K Q
♣ 8 7 3

♠ Q 9 5   N   ♠ K 8 7 4
♡ A 5   W   E   ♡ 8
◇ 10 6 5 4 3   S   ◇ A J 9 2
♣ J 10 5   ♣ Q 9 6 4

♠ 6 2
♡ K Q 10 9 4 3
◇ 8 7
♣ A K 2

West leads the jack of clubs against your heart game. If you win the opening lead and set about drawing trumps, what do you think will happen?

Right — West will take the ace of hearts and play a second club. You will be able to extract the last of the defenders' trumps, but there is nothing you can then do to avoid losing a trick in each side suit: one down!

On this deal you cannot afford the luxury of starting trumps immediately. You must first address the problem of having too many losers. You cannot avoid losing the two red aces and a spade, so your need to dispose of your third club before the defenders can score a trick in that suit.

Win the opening lead and immediately play a spade. If West follows with a low card, play the ♠10 from dummy. East wins and returns a second club, which you win. Again, you cannot afford to play trumps yet, so you lead a second spade. You repeat the finesse and dummy's ♠J wins the trick. You can now cash the ♠A to dispose of the third club from your hand.

Having side-stepped the third plain-suit loser, you can now turn your attention to knocking out the ace of trumps.

Did you notice that West could have beaten your contract? See what happens if he steps in with the ♠Q when you lead the first round of the suit towards dummy: you can set up a spade winner easily enough, but with no fast entry to dummy you will be unable to reach it in time. Fortunately, though, few defenders play that well even at the very highest level.

Had dummy's spades been slightly better, say A-Q-10, the defenders would then be unable to stop you from taking two finesses and (assuming West holds one of the missing honors) disposing of your club loser.

2.

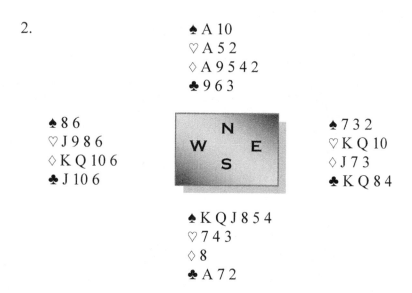

```
                    ♠ A 10
                    ♡ A 5 2
                    ◊ A 9 5 4 2
                    ♣ 9 6 3

 ♠ 8 6                               ♠ 7 3 2
 ♡ J 9 8 6          N                ♡ K Q 10
 ◊ K Q 10 6     W       E            ◊ J 7 3
 ♣ J 10 6           S                ♣ K Q 8 4

                    ♠ K Q J 8 5 4
                    ♡ 7 4 3
                    ◊ 8
                    ♣ A 7 2
```

West leads the ◊K against your Four Spade contract.

A quick count of your losers reveals one more than you can afford – two hearts and two clubs. How might you dispose of one of these?

The only possibility is to establish the long diamond as a winner if the defenders' cards in that suit break 4-3, but entries to dummy are limited. If you play even one round of trumps before setting about ruffing diamonds, you will no longer be able to make the contract.

The plan is to win the ◊A and immediately ruff a diamond, You can then return to dummy with the ♠10 and ruff another diamond. Drawing a second round of trumps with the ♠A gets us back to dummy for a third time, enabling you to take a third diamond ruff, setting up the thirteenth card in the suit as a winner.

You can now draw the defenders' last trump. The ♡A provides access to the long diamond, on which you can dispose of one of your four rounded-suit losers.

On this deal, we needed exactly four entries to dummy – three to take ruffs and a fourth in order to cash the established winner. It was also vital that the first of the four available entries used was the ◇A, so an opening lead of either major would have defeated this contract. (On a club lead, you could essentially follow the same line of play by winning the ace and crossing to the ace of diamonds at trick two.)

Luckily, the defenders will not always find the best lead against you. When they fail to do so, though, it is important that you take advantage.

Chapter 4 – The Crossruff

Thus far, we have concentrated on the question of WHEN to draw trumps, the assumption being that even if you have something else to do first you will eventually do so. On some deals, though, you make a conscious decision not to draw trumps at all but, instead, to try scoring your trumps separately by taking ruffs in both hands – welcome to the crossruff.

Take a look at this deal:

Both Vul: Dealer South

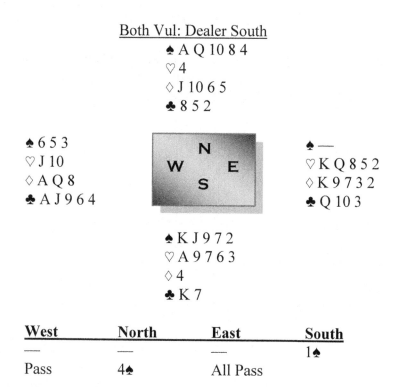

♠ A Q 10 8 4
♡ 4
♢ J 10 6 5
♣ 8 5 2

♠ 6 5 3
♡ J 10
♢ A Q 8
♣ A J 9 6 4

♠ —
♡ K Q 8 5 2
♢ K 9 7 3 2
♣ Q 10 3

♠ K J 9 7 2
♡ A 9 7 6 3
♢ 4
♣ K 7

West	North	East	South
—	—	—	1♠
Pass	4♠	All Pass	

West leads the jack of hearts against your Four Spade contract. How do you play?

Ask yourself 'Do I have enough tricks to make my contract if I draw trumps?' The answer here is not a clear "Yes". The ace of clubs

65

may be onside and hearts might split 4-3, but you would surely rather not rely on such things. Shortages in both your hand and dummy should suggest you think of playing on a crossruff.

Win the ♡A, ruff a heart and lead a diamond, creating an easy route back to your hand. West wins and switches to a trump but you are in control: win in hand and ruff a heart. Now ruff a diamond to get back to your hand. Heart ruff, diamond ruff, heart ruff, diamond ruff brings your tally of tricks to ten via nine trumps and the ace of hearts.

Many players would fall into the trap of leading a club towards the king at trick three. When the ♣K loses, West will switch to a trump with fatal consequences. Declarer can win in hand and ruff a second heart but then has no quick route back to hand: West cannot be stopped from gaining the lead again and he will play a second round of trumps, leaving declarer a trick short.

Accurate timing is often vital on crossruff deals, so you may need to foresee the later play in order to lay the necessary groundwork early. Cover the E/W hands and take a look at this deal:

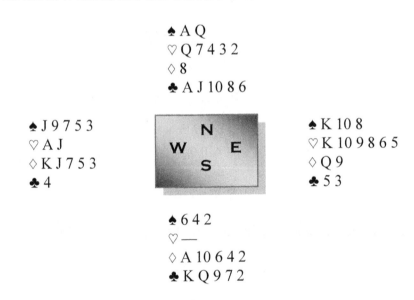

```
                 ♠ A Q
                 ♡ Q 7 4 3 2
                 ◇ 8
                 ♣ A J 10 8 6

  ♠ J 9 7 5 3          N          ♠ K 10 8
  ♡ A J            W        E      ♡ K 10 9 8 6 5
  ◇ K J 7 5 3          S          ◇ Q 9
  ♣ 4                             ♣ 5 3

                 ♠ 6 4 2
                 ♡ —
                 ◇ A 10 6 4 2
                 ♣ K Q 9 7 2
```

West opens One Spade and North cue-bids Two Spades showing at least 5-5 in hearts and a minor. East attempts to get in the way with a raise to Three Spades but you brush him aside and quickly reach Six Clubs. West leads the ♠5. How would you play?

Let's start by counting our tricks. West's opening bid makes it likely that he will hold the ♠K, and a winning finesse would give you two spade tricks. If you can draw trumps in two rounds and then find the defenders' diamonds breaking 4-3, you can just about see your way to twelve tricks. Does that not seem like rather too many 'ifs', though? Indeed, if you take a spade finesse on this layout, East will win and return a trump leaving you with no chance.

Aiming to score all of your trumps separately to go along with two outside aces looks like a better plan. The objective is to ruff all of dummy's hearts in hand using diamond ruffs as entries to dummy.

The timing is important: you must win the ♠A at trick one and immediately ruff a heart. You can then cash the ◊A and set about your crossruff. The alternative of playing a diamond to the ace at trick two does not work as you will eventually find yourself in the wrong hand.

The deal above had all the hallmarks that should lead you to think of playing a crossruff – a big trump fit and side-suit shortages in both hands. Our next deal, though, has neither of those elements.

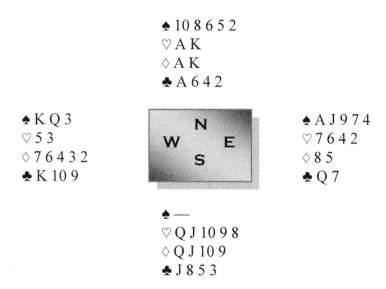

```
              ♠ 10 8 6 5 2
              ♡ A K
              ◊ A K
              ♣ A 6 4 2

♠ K Q 3                          ♠ A J 9 7 4
♡ 5 3            N               ♡ 7 6 4 2
◊ 7 6 4 3 2   W     E            ◊ 8 5
♣ K 10 9        S               ♣ Q 7

              ♠ —
              ♡ Q J 10 9 8
              ◊ Q J 10 9
              ♣ J 8 5 3
```

You bid well, avoiding the doomed 3NT and instead land in Four Hearts. West leads the ♠K. How will you play?

When you count tricks, it would be easy to conclude that you have five trumps, four diamonds and the ♣A for a total of ten. However, let's see what happens if you ruff the opening spade lead and then make what looks like the natural play of cashing dummy's top trumps.

Having then unblocked the diamonds, the only route back to your hand is via another spade ruff, with your penultimate trump. When you then cash your last trump, though, West discards. The only other trick you can make is the ace of clubs: two down.

This line of play needs the defenders' trumps to split 3-3. When they do not, you can score only two diamond tricks rather than the four you had anticipated. In fact, though, the contract can be made irrespective of how trumps divide as long as neither defender is able ruff one of your minor-suit winners.

The solidity of the diamonds acted as a smokescreen to confuse declarer here. The winning line of play would have been easier to see if you had held four low diamonds rather than the Queen-Jack. Having ruffed the opening spade lead, cash dummy's top diamonds and the ♣A. You can then ruff a spade, ruff a diamond with the ♡K, ruff another spade, ruff your last diamond with the ♡A, and claim two more tricks with high trumps. You have made seven trump tricks to go with three winners in the minors – ten tricks and contract made.

Now you've got the idea, take a shot at a slam hand. Cover the E/W cards if you want to test yourself before reading on:

$$\begin{array}{l} \spadesuit\text{A 8 6 5 2} \\ \heartsuit\text{J 9 8 6} \\ \diamondsuit\text{A K 4} \\ \clubsuit\text{4} \end{array}$$

♠ K Q J 10 9 3		♠ 7
♡ —		♡ 7 5 4 2
◇ Q 10 9 6 3		◇ J 8
♣ Q 9		♣ K J 10 7 6 2

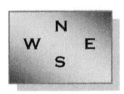

$$\begin{array}{l} \spadesuit\text{4} \\ \heartsuit\text{A K Q 10 3} \\ \diamondsuit\text{7 5 2} \\ \clubsuit\text{A 8 5 3} \end{array}$$

You open One Heart, West overcalls Four Spades, and your partner Blackwoods you to slam. West leads the ♠K against Six Hearts and when you play dummy's ace you are relieved to see East follow suit. How do you continue?

If your first inclination is to draw trumps, go back and count your losers again: you have one diamond loser and three clubs. You cannot avoid losing the third round of diamonds so you will need to dispose of all three club losers and that can only be done by ruffing them in dummy. Alternatively, you can count your tricks: with four side-suit winners available, you will need to score eight trump tricks, five in hand and three club ruffs in dummy.

Let's see how the play might go: the ace of spades is followed by a club to the ace and a club ruff. You now cross to hand with a spade ruff (East discarding a diamond) and ruff another club. A second spade ruff puts you back in hand to ruff your last club. You now return to hand using dummy's last trump. Oops! West discards, so East started with four trumps, which is one more than you have left. You can cash your remaining trumps, but when you then play a diamond to the ace, North ruffs and cashes club winners: two down.

What went wrong? You scored the two black-suit aces and the eight trump tricks you needed. However, you didn't make a single diamond trick. Here is an important rule to remember: "When embarking on a crossruff, cash your side-suit winners before the defenders can make damaging discards".

Let's go back to beginning. Having won the opening lead with the ♠A, your first move should be to cash dummy's top diamonds. With those tricks safely in the bag, you can now set about your crossruff — ♣A, club ruff, spade ruff, club ruff, spade ruff, club ruff, trump to hand. You are left with two high trumps and a diamond loser: twelve tricks.

Quiz Hands

1. <u>None Vul: Dealer South</u>

♠ 4
♡ A J 8 6 5
♢ 8 5 3
♣ A Q 9 6

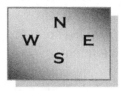

♠ A J 6 3
♡ 4 3
♢ A 7
♣ K J 8 5 2

West	North	East	South
—	—	—	1♣
1♠	2♡	2♠	Pass
4♠	5♣	All Pass	

West leads the ♢K against your Five Clubs.
How should you play?

2.　　　　　　E/W Game: Dealer South
　　　　　　　♠ A 10 8 4
　　　　　　　♡ K 6 5
　　　　　　　◇ A J 8 5 3
　　　　　　　♣ 6

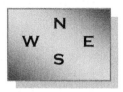

　　　　　♠ K Q J 6
　　　　　♡ 9 4 3
　　　　　◇ 7
　　　　　♣ A Q 7 4 2

West	North	East	South
—	—	—	1♣
Pass	1◇	Pass	1♠
Pass	4♠	All Pass	

West leads the ♡Q against your spade game.

The ♡A is clearly offside, so your only chance of scoring a trick in the suit is to find East with a singleton or doubleton ace. You play low from dummy at trick one, and duck again when West continues with the ♡J. The ace still has not appeared, and West leads a third heart to dummy's king and East's ace. East then returns a trump.

How do you play?

1.

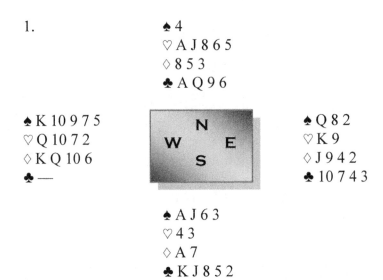

♠ 4
♡ A J 8 6 5
◊ 8 5 3
♣ A Q 9 6

♠ K 10 9 7 5
♡ Q 10 7 2
◊ K Q 10 6
♣ —

♠ Q 8 2
♡ K 9
◊ J 9 4 2
♣ 10 7 4 3

♠ A J 6 3
♡ 4 3
◊ A 7
♣ K J 8 5 2

You bid to Five Clubs over the opponents' Four Spades and West leads the king of diamonds.

Although you have contracted for an 11-trick game, you have very few winners outside the trump suit. This situation is often an indicator that you should attempt a crossruff in order to maximize the number of trump tricks you make.

Before you can crossruff, though, you will first have to give up a heart trick. If you make the mistake of cashing even one round of trumps before relinquishing the lead, East will be able to play another trump when he gets in with the ♡K. There will then be no way to come to eleven tricks.

Win the opening lead with the ◊A, cash the ♠A and ruff a spade in dummy. Next, play the ♡A and give up a heart. East can win, cash his jack of diamonds, and switch to a trump, but you will be able to score your remaining trumps separately. Three side-suit aces and eight trump tricks (five club winners in your hand and three spade ruffs in dummy) add up to eleven.

2.

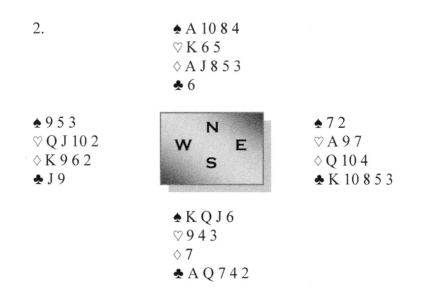

♠ A 10 8 4
♥ K 6 5
♦ A J 8 5 3
♣ 6

♠ 9 5 3
♥ Q J 10 2
♦ K 9 6 2
♣ J 9

♠ 7 2
♥ A 9 7
♦ Q 10 4
♣ K 10 8 5 3

♠ K Q J 6
♥ 9 4 3
♦ 7
♣ A Q 7 4 2

You bid unopposed to Four Spades. The defenders start with three rounds of hearts, killing dummy's king, and then switch to a trump. How should you play?

A singleton in both declarer's hand and dummy often suggests that a crossruff may be possible. However, before embarking on such a line of play you need to count your tricks: one trump trick, three ruffs in each hand and two aces only totals nine – you are a trick short.

Barring a very fortunate lie of the cards (a doubleton K-Q of diamonds, for example), you will end up with a loser at the end after scoring all of your remaining trumps separately. There is also the small chance that the ♣K will fall in three rounds, but that is not a favorite either (since you will also need trumps to split 3-2).

What can be done?

The only way to bring home your game is to grit your teeth and take the club finesse: win the trump switch in dummy and play a club to the queen. When that finesse wins, cash the minor-suit aces and cross-ruff the rest of the tricks. (If West holds the ♣K, then the odds are that you were going down no matter what you did.)

Note that if you had stopped in Three Spades, it would then be wrong to take the club finesse. If you do, and it loses, West could then return a second trump, leaving you with only eight tricks.

Chapter 5 – Keeping Control

Why choose a trump suit? One of the primary reasons is so that you can prevent the defenders from cashing winners in another suit. How do you assess your prospects on this slam hand?

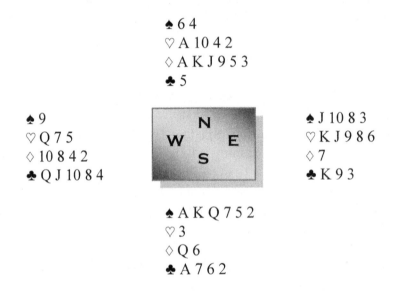

```
                    ♠ 6 4
                    ♡ A 10 4 2
                    ◊ A K J 9 5 3
                    ♣ 5

  ♠ 9                  N             ♠ J 10 8 3
  ♡ Q 7 5         W         E        ♡ K J 9 8 6
  ◊ 10 8 4 2           S             ◊ 7
  ♣ Q J 10 8 4                       ♣ K 9 3

                    ♠ A K Q 7 5 2
                    ♡ 3
                    ◊ Q 6
                    ♣ A 7 6 2
```

West attacks with the ♣Q against your Six Spade contract. How would you play?

Perhaps your immediate reaction when you see dummy is that you have missed an easy grand slam. Such thoughts, though, are only likely to distract you from the task in hand, making twelve tricks.

With all of those diamond winners in dummy, you have plenty of tricks, so it seems clear that you should start drawing trumps immediately. When a contract looks easy, though, you should always take a moment to ask yourself is "What could go wrong?"

If you start by cashing two high trumps and either opponent shows out, you will almost certainly go down. Try playing it through.

A better option is to ruff a club, cross back to hand with the ◊Q and ruff a second club. You can then re-enter your hand with a heart ruff and cash the three top trumps. If either defender holds four trumps and a singleton diamond, though, this line will also fail.

Your primary objective should be to safeguard your contract against the not insignificant chance that the trumps will break 4-1, which will happen almost one third of the time. Since you will have to give up a trick in the suit if a defender holds four trumps, you should make sure you do so when it is safe — that means when there is still a trump in dummy to deal with a club continuation.

The best option is to lead a low trump from your hand at trick two. Sure, two-thirds of the time you are giving up an overtrick, but this is a small investment to pay for virtually ensuring the success of a slam contract. (This line of play fails only against some 5-0 trump breaks that would likely also defeat other lines too.)

Sometimes you can set about drawing trumps and then reassess that strategy once you see how the suit splits.

Both Vul: Dealer East

♠ A J 7
♡ 9 8 4
◇ A K 9 3
♣ K 9 5

♠ 3		♠ 8 6 4 2
♡ Q 6 5	**N**	♡ A K J 10 3
◇ 8 2	**W**　**E**	◇ Q 7 5
♣ Q 10 8 7 6 4 3	**S**	♣ J

♠ K Q 10 9 5
♡ 7 2
◇ J 10 6 4
♣ A 2

West	North	East	South
—	—	1♡	1♠
2♡	4♠	All Pass	

The defense begins with three rounds of hearts against your spade game.

What is your plan?

With a potential diamond still to be lost, you have little option but to ruff the third round of hearts. You immediately set about drawing trumps, playing the ace and a second round won in your hand, but West discards a club meaning that East now has the same number of trumps left as you.

If you were to now draw the remaining trumps, you would then be reliant on avoiding a diamond loser. If East is able to win a diamond trick, he will be able to cash two more heart winners. How can you avoid this fate?

The answer is to knock out East's potential diamond stopper while dummy still controls the heart suit. You must run the ◊J after cashing only two rounds of trumps. You do not care even if this loses to a singleton queen, since that will be the third and last trick for the defense.

East wins with the ◊Q but he cannot shorten the trumps in your hand: if he plays another heart, you can ruff in dummy. You will then cross to hand in clubs and remove his trumps before cashing the rest of your diamond winners.

By leaving trumps outstanding while you set up the side suit tricks needed to fulfill your contract, you were able to retain control of the trump suit despite the bad break.

Note that it is important which trumps you use to draw the first two rounds. Firstly, you want to be in hand after two rounds of trumps so that you can finesse in diamonds if trumps don't behave. (If you are in dummy and have to play diamonds from the top, you may go down even with the ◊Q onside.) You also want to avoid blocking the suit, so do not leave dummy with the bare ace. However, dummy must keep a high trump so that it can overruff West on the fourth round of hearts if that proves necessary.

So, after two rounds of trumps the lead should be in your hand with the lone ♠J left in dummy.

Our next deal has a similar theme:

```
              ♠ Q 9 4
              ♡ K 4 2
              ◇ 10 7 3
              ♣ K Q 10 5

♠ 8 7 3 2                            ♠ 6
♡ J 9              N                 ♡ Q 10 8 6 5
◇ K Q J 8      W       E             ◇ A 9 5 4 2
♣ A 8 4            S                 ♣ 7 3

              ♠ A K J 10 5
              ♡ A 7 3
              ◇ 6
              ♣ J 9 6 2
```

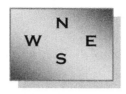

You reach Four Spades in an uncontested auction and West kicks things off with the king and queen of diamonds. How should you play?

You ruff the second round of diamonds and start drawing trumps by cashing the king and jack. As a matter of general technique, when you have high trumps of equal value in both your hand and dummy, you should get into the habit of cashing them in a way that retains the flexibility to win any specific round (the third here) in either your hand or dummy.

If both defenders follow twice, you plan to draw the last trump and knock out the ace of clubs to establish your ten tricks. Today, though, East discards a heart on the second round of trumps.

You now know that West holds the same number of trumps as you. If you draw even one more round of trumps, you will have surrendered control and the contract will eventually fail: When the defenders gain the lead with the ♣A, they will force you to ruff with your last trump by continuing diamonds. You still have an unavoidable heart loser and West's 'long' trump will then be the defenders' fourth trick.

Instead, you must drive out the ace of clubs immediately. If the defenders allow you to win the first round of clubs, you have to continue with a second round. Yes, you risk running into a club ruff,

77

but you have to take that chance since you already know that any other line of play leads to certain defeat.

You are not quite home yet, though: suppose West wins the second round of clubs and leads another high diamond. What will you do?

If you ruff, you will again have lost trump control. You will eventually have to lose a heart anyway, so simply throw that loser on the third round of diamonds. Dummy's remaining trump now does for you what Yoda and company did for young Luke Skywalker, protects you from the force.

Whatever West does now, you will be able to finish drawing trumps and then cash your established winners.

The objective on the previous two deals was to avoid having your trumps shortened, thus stopping a defender gaining control of the trump suit. On our next deal, the defenders are threatening your trump holding in a different way. Can you see how to halt their dastardly plan?

Both Vul: Dealer North

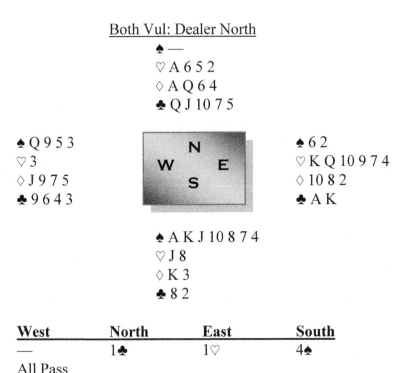

```
                  ♠ —
                  ♡ A 6 5 2
                  ◊ A Q 6 4
                  ♣ Q J 10 7 5

♠ Q 9 5 3            N            ♠ 6 2
♡ 3            W         E        ♡ K Q 10 9 7 4
◊ J 9 7 5            S            ◊ 10 8 2
♣ 9 6 4 3                         ♣ A K

                  ♠ A K J 10 8 7 4
                  ♡ J 8
                  ◊ K 3
                  ♣ 8 2
```

West	North	East	South
—	1♣	1♡	4♠
All Pass			

Your pragmatic Four Spade bid concludes a brief auction and West leads the ♡3.

How do you play?

West's lead of the lowest missing heart marks him with a singleton, so you are obliged to take your ♡A right away. You then cross to the ♢K and cash your top trumps in the hope that the queen will fall, but today is not your birthday.

If you play a third round of trumps to drive out the queen at this stage, the defense will surely cash two clubs and a heart to defeat your contract out of hand. You must first dispose of one of those three side-suit losers before letting the opponents in, so you cross to the ♢A and pitch one of your clubs on dummy's remaining high diamond.

You then lead dummy's last diamond on which East discards a heart. You know that West is going to follow to the fourth round of diamonds, so does that mean it is safe for you to ruff and lead the ♠J to force out the queen?

Let's see what happens: West wins with the trump queen and plays a club to his partner's king. East now cashes his heart winner and continues with a third round of the suit. You can ruff, but so can West behind you. That third round of hearts has promoted West's ♠9 into the setting trick.

To counter this you needed to find a way to keep East off lead. Your chance to achieve that goal came when you led the fourth round of diamonds from dummy and East showed out. Rather than ruffing that trick, notice the difference if instead you discard your second club.

Although West will win an apparently cheap trick with the ♢J, you have severed the defensive communications. No matter what West does next, you will be able to drive out his queen of trumps, regain the lead again, and draw the fourth round of trumps. You will have to give East a trick at the end with his heart winner, but that is the third and last defensive trick: contract made.

Your trump holding on the previous deal looked adequate and yet it was endangered by a not-unlikely distribution. It is easy to think your trump suit is more robust than it is. Take a look at this next deal:

None Vul: Dealer South

```
                    ♠ J 5 4
                    ♡ K 6 2
                    ◇ Q 10 8 6 2
                    ♣ A 7

♠ A K 10 9 6 2           N              ♠ 8 3
♡ 10 7 4 3         W         E          ♡ 9
◇ 9 5                   S              ◇ A J 7 4 3
♣ 4                                    ♣ 9 8 6 3 2

                    ♠ Q 7
                    ♡ A Q J 8 5
                    ◇ K
                    ♣ K Q J 10 5
```

West	North	East	South
—	—	Pass	1♡
2♠	3♡	Pass	4♡
All Pass			

Three No Trumps would have been impregnable, but you quite understandably reach game in your 8-card major-suit fit. Against Four Hearts, West opens the defense with three rounds of spades, East ruffing dummy's jack with the ♡9.

Your trumps look more than capable of withstanding this assault but, if you make the mistake of overruffing you will soon discover that West's ♡10 has been promoted into the setting trick. Yes, it is rather unlucky to find the pre-emptor with a 4-card holding in the other major, but that is no excuse for carelessness. Discard your losing king of diamonds at trick three and the remaining tricks will be yours.

The opponents could have prevailed legitimately had they cashed their diamond winner before uppercutting your trumps, but that is a tough sequence of plays for them to find. Do not allow them to defeat you with the second-best defense.

On the last couple of deals, you have been able to discard a loser as an alternative to weakening your trump holding. On the next layout, many declarers would go down before they even realized that they had reached the decision point of the deal. See if you can spot the solution:

E/W Game: Dealer East

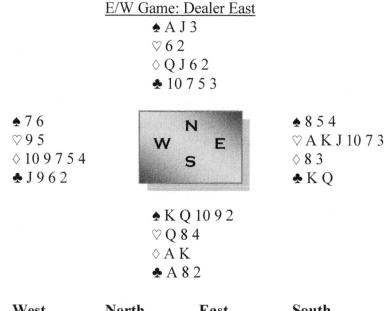

♠ A J 3
♡ 6 2
◊ Q J 6 2
♣ 10 7 5 3

♠ 7 6
♡ 9 5
◊ 10 9 7 5 4
♣ J 9 6 2

♠ 8 5 4
♡ A K J 10 7 3
◊ 8 3
♣ K Q

♠ K Q 10 9 2
♡ Q 8 4
◊ A K
♣ A 8 2

West	North	East	South
—	—	1♡	1♠
Pass	2♠	Pass	4♠
All Pass			

West leads the ♡9 and East cashes the ace and king. A third heart goes to your queen and West ruffs with the ♠6. How do you play?

You have nothing useful to discard from dummy on this trick and your trump suit is solid, so overruffing cannot promote a trump trick for the defense. Can you see any reason not to overruff?

You have already lost two heart tricks and thus you must avoid losing two clubs. How are you planning to achieve this?

The only realistic chance is to discard the losing clubs on dummy's diamonds, but your sole entry to those winners lies in the trump suit. If you overruff the third heart, you will not then be able to draw three rounds of trumps finishing in dummy. You can unblock the ace and king of diamonds and draw two trumps ending in dummy, but when East ruffs the next diamond your goose will be well and truly cooked.

Although in itself it achieves nothing material, you must discard a club and allow West's small trump to score at trick three. You will then be able to win West's return and draw two rounds of trumps (keeping a winner in dummy). Having unblocked the ◇A-K, you can then draw East's last trump, crossing to dummy in the process. You can now safely discard your two losing clubs on dummy's queen-jack of diamonds.

Giving a ruff-and-sluff is usually poor defense. If declarer has no loser to dispose of, though, it can be an effective way of attacking his trump holding. Cover the E/W cards and see how you would cope with East's defensive ploy on this deal:

<u>None Vul: Dealer East</u>

```
                  ♠ Q 5 4
                  ♡ Q 8
                  ◇ 10 6 2
                  ♣ A Q J 7 5

  ♠ 3                              ♠ K 8 6 2
  ♡ 10 9 7 5 4 3       N           ♡ 6
  ◇ 9 5            W        E       ◇ A K Q J 7
  ♣ K 9 4 3            S           ♣ 10 8 6

                  ♠ A J 10 9 7
                  ♡ A K J 2
                  ◇ 8 4 3
                  ♣ 2
```

West	North	East	South
—	—	1◇	1♠
Pass	2◇	Pass	4♠
All Pass			

You brush aside East's One Diamond opening bid to reach Four Spades. West leads the ◇9 and East cashes three winners in the suit, West discarding a heart on the third round. How do you play when East then continues with a fourth round of diamonds?

We have established the general principle of taking ruffs in the short trump hand and using the long hand to keep control and draw the enemy trumps. Suppose you follow the rule here and ruff the fourth diamond in dummy. You then play the trump queen and successfully run it. You can repeat the winning finesse but, when West discards, you cannot then pick up East's remaining K-x of trumps.

You have no useful discard on the fourth round of diamonds, so you should focus on the trump suit itself. By ruffing the fourth diamond in the long trump hand you retain dummy's trump length so that you can nullify East's trump king even though he has a four-card holding. Having ruffed the fourth diamond with the ♠9, cross to dummy with the ♡Q, run the ♠Q, and then take a second trump finesse. West discards but you can re-enter dummy with the ♣A and lead a third trump, finessing again to avoid losing a trump trick.

Rules are made to be broken, and on this occasion it was length in the short trump hand that needed to be preserved in order to keep control of the suit.

Leading trumps at the right time can be tricky when you hold a two-suited hand. See if you can bring home a lowly partscore contract on our next deal:

               ♠ K Q 8
               ♡ A K 4
               ◊ J 7 5
               ♣ 8 7 5 2

♠ 7 3   ♠ A 6 4
♡ J 8 7   ♡ Q 9 6 5 2
◊ A Q 8   ◊ K 9
♣ K J 9 6 4   ♣ Q 10 3

               ♠ J 10 9 5 2
               ♡ 10 3
               ◊ 10 6 4 3 2
               ♣ A

In a competitive auction, E/W bid to Three Clubs and you soldier on to Three Spades. West leads the ♣6. How do you play?

You can count only seven tricks, four trumps in hand and three top winners outside. If you set about trumps immediately and the defenders simply keep leading clubs each time they gain the lead, you will quickly run out of trumps. However, the prospect of establishing and cashing diamond tricks looks like a hopeless task since you will have to lose the lead four times (three times in diamonds and once in trumps).

Inexperienced players often find this type of deal particularly difficult to time. The general rule is that when you hold a two-suited hand you should set about the establishment of the side suit first, and this deal is no exception.

American football fans will understand the concept of the option play: the quarterback (QB) carries the ball with a running back (RB) outside and only one defender in front of them. If the defender moves outside to guard the RB, the quarterback keeps the ball and runs in for a touchdown. If the defender moves inside to tackle the QB, then he flips the ball to his teammate (the option), who scores in the corner of the endzone. Whatever move the defensive player makes, the offense has a winning option. On this deal, declarer can put E/W in the position of that defensive player, with two available choices, neither of them successful.

Suppose declarer leads a diamond at trick two, taken by East with the king. If East switches to a low trump, declarer wins in dummy and leads a second diamond. West wins with the ◇Q and plays a second trump to his partner's ace and East exits with a third round of trumps. Declarer wins and leads a third round of diamonds to West's ace. Now the defense leads a second round of clubs, but declarer ruffs and cashes two winning diamonds. Declarer makes four trumps in hand, two top hearts, the ace of clubs and two long diamonds to bring his total to nine tricks.

Drawing trumps does not seem to be a successful strategy for the defense, so how about playing a forcing game? Perhaps they can run declarer out of trumps and therefore cut him off from those long diamonds. As before, then, declarer wins the opening club lead with the ace and leads a diamond taken by East with the king. This time,

East returns a second club and declarer ruffs. A second diamond is won by the queen and West perseveres with a third round of clubs. Again declarer ruffs.

The defenders have succeeded in their objective in that although declarer can establish two diamond winners he will never be able to reach them. However, it is now that declarer flips the ball out to the running back – the option!

The defenders have made you ruff twice already, so now is the time to switch strategies and continue the work they have started. Cross to dummy in hearts and lead dummy's fourth club. East cannot profitably ruff, so he pitches a heart and you ruff. You then re-enter dummy once more in hearts in order to take a heart ruff. You have already scored three high-card tricks in the side suits plus four ruffs in your hand.

You can now exit with your last trump, the jack. Dummy's ♠K-Q still remain, giving you a total of six trump tricks to go with your three outside winners: nine tricks again.

Quiz Hands

1.

None Vul: Dealer East

♠ Q 10 3
♡ A 9 6 2
◇ J 6 2
♣ K 7 3

♠ A K J 2
♡ 8 7 4
◇ 4
♣ A Q J 4 2

West	North	East	South
—	—	Pass	1♣
1◇	1♡	2◇	2♠
3◇	3♠	Pass	4♡
Pass	4♠	All Pass	

The opponents' diamond bidding steers you away from notrumps, but your partner still shows good judgment to avoid the hopeless minor-suit game in preference for Four Spades on a 4-3 fit.

West opens the defense with a high diamond and continues the suit. How do you play?

2.

♠ A K 6 5 3
♡ K 2
◇ Q J 2
♣ 8 7 5

♠ 9 7
♡ A J 10 9 4
◇ A K 9 6 4
♣ 2

West	North	East	South
—	—		1♡
3♣	3♠	Pass	4◇
Pass	4♡	All Pass	

West pre-empts in clubs at unfavorable vulnerability and your side is again left with a choice between an 11-trick game in an 8-card fit or a major-suit contract with only seven trumps.

You opt to play Four Hearts and West opens proceedings with the ace and king of clubs.

How do you play?

Answers to Quiz Hands

1.

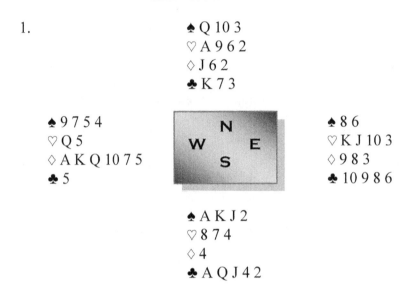

♠ Q 10 3
♡ A 9 6 2
◇ J 6 2
♣ K 7 3

♠ 9 7 5 4
♡ Q 5
◇ A K Q 10 7 5
♣ 5

♠ 8 6
♡ K J 10 3
◇ 9 8 3
♣ 10 9 8 6

♠ A K J 2
♡ 8 7 4
◇ 4
♣ A Q J 4 2

You landed in the only game contract with a chance of making, but you will need to be careful playing in the 4-3 spade fit.

You can count ten tricks (five clubs, four spades and one heart) provided you keep control of the trump suit. West leads the king of diamonds and continues with the queen at trick two. After ruffing the second round of diamonds, you try to draw trumps but when the suit fails to break evenly you are in trouble. West is left with the last trump: you will be able to cash only one club trick before he ruffs in and produces an avalanche of diamond winners.

You have losing hearts, so simply discard one of those and let West's ◇Q win trick two. When he persists with a third high diamond, repeat the process by pitching your second losing heart.

Whatever West leads at trick four you can win as dummy's high trumps protect you from a fourth round of diamonds. As soon as you gain the lead you can set about drawing trumps. The suit splits 4-2, but that is okay: because you preserved your trump length, you are able to draw all of the defenders' trumps and claim your contract.

2.

$\spadesuit$ A K 6 5 3
$\heartsuit$ K 2
$\diamondsuit$ Q J 2
$\clubsuit$ 8 7 5

$\spadesuit$ J 8
$\heartsuit$ Q 7 5 3
$\diamondsuit$ 7
$\clubsuit$ A K Q J 9 4

$\spadesuit$ Q 10 4 2
$\heartsuit$ 9 6
$\diamondsuit$ 10 8 5 3
$\clubsuit$ 10 6 3

$\spadesuit$ 9 7
$\heartsuit$ A J 10 9 4
$\diamondsuit$ A K 9 6 4
$\clubsuit$ 2

West	North	East	South
—	—		1$\heartsuit$
3$\clubsuit$	3$\spadesuit$	Pass	4$\diamondsuit$
Pass	4$\heartsuit$	All Pass	

Despite the vulnerability, West pre-empts in clubs after your One Heart opening bid. You eventually land in Four Hearts and West kicks off the defense with two high clubs.

Nothing can be gained by failing to ruff the second round of clubs. Having begun with only a 7-card trump fit, though, you are acutely aware that losing control is a serious danger.

With West known to hold at least six clubs, East is a favorite to hold the $\heartsuit$Q. A little learning can be a dangerous thing, though: suppose you play a trump to dummy's king at trick two, and finesse against East on the way back. When West wins with the queen of trumps and leads a third round of clubs, forcing you to ruff with your penultimate trump, you are in serious trouble. You cash the ace of trumps hoping to drop both of the outstanding trumps. When East shows out, though, your fate is sealed.

You can cash two spades and one diamond trick, but West will claim the rest of the tricks with the thirteenth trump and a slew of clubs.

Sure, it was unfortunate to find the pre-emptor with four trumps, but you cannot put this poor result down to bad luck.

Let's go back and count tricks: you have five diamonds and two spades, so you need to make only three trump tricks. Yes, you can afford to lose two trumps. If you draw two rounds of trumps with the ace and king, you just need both defenders to follow suit twice. If the queen of trumps has not appeared, you now start cashing diamonds whilst still in control of the trump suit. You are quite happy for the defenders to score their remaining two trumps separately, irrespective of how they are divided and who holds the queen.

Chapter 6 – Avoiding Ruffs

Judging when to draw trumps is usually the most important decision you make when planning the play in a suit contract. There can be numerous benefits to playing in a suit contract rather than in notrumps but there is, of course, one major disadvantage too: the defenders may be able to ruff one or more of your winners.

As beginners, a number of general principles are drummed into us and, for the most part, simply following those guidelines stands us in good stead. All rules have exceptions, though, and there is no substitute for actually thinking. Take a look at this deal:

♠ J 4
♡ A 6 3
◇ A K J 10 3
♣ 7 5 4

♠ K Q 5		♠ 10 9 8 6 3 2
♡ J 9 8 7	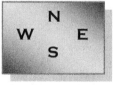	♡ 10
◇ 8 3		◇ 9 8 7 2
♣ A J 9 3		♣ Q 10

♠ A 7
♡ K Q 5 4 2
◇ Q 5
♣ K 8 6 2

An uncontested auction carries you to Four Hearts against which West leads the ♠K. How do you play?

You have plenty of winners, so you should start by drawing trumps. When you cash your second high heart, East shows out, but that's still okay: four hearts, five diamonds and one spade still adds up to ten.

After cashing your three high trumps, you start on diamonds. Alas, West ruffs the third round of diamonds, cashes the ♠Q, and plays a third spade. You have to ruff and must subsequently lose three club tricks since you now have no entry to dummy's long diamonds.

Whilst it is usually correct to leave an opponent with a high trump rather than playing an extra round of the suit, there is one notable exception – when you have a long suit to cash but no outside entry to it. After winning the ♠A at trick one, simply play four rounds of trumps, giving West his winner at a time convenient to you. West can cash his spade trick and the defenders will make the ♣A (either then or later), but your contract is safe.

You may not be able to prevent a defender scoring a trump trick, but WHEN he takes that trick may determine the success or failure of your contract. Our next deal is a variation on this theme. Cover the E/W cards and see if you can spot how to bring home your slam:

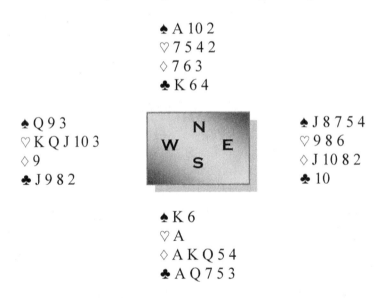

```
              ♠ A 10 2
              ♡ 7 5 4 2
              ◇ 7 6 3
              ♣ K 6 4

♠ Q 9 3          N          ♠ J 8 7 5 4
♡ K Q J 10 3   W   E        ♡ 9 8 6
◇ 9              S          ◇ J 10 8 2
♣ J 9 8 2                   ♣ 10

              ♠ K 6
              ♡ A
              ◇ A K Q 5 4
              ♣ A Q 7 5 3
```

You reach Six Diamonds and West leads the ♡K.

If both minor suits split 3-2, you will have thirteen tricks, but when you cash two high trumps West discards. How do you continue?

You can do nothing about East's trump trick, but your contract will still be safe if clubs break. What if clubs are also 4-1, though?

You need to test the clubs while dummy still has a trump. If East also holds four clubs, you will then be able to ruff the fourth round in dummy while he has to follow suit. What if East has a singleton club, though? If you play the ace and king of clubs, East will ruff and return his last trump. You will still have to lose a club to West later.

The key is to lead the second round of clubs through East: play a club to dummy's king and a second club towards the honors in your hand. If both defenders follow suit, you can cash the last high trump and claim twelve tricks. If East started with only one club, though, it will not help him to ruff. You win with the ♣A and repeat the process: cross back to dummy with the ace of spades and lead the third round of clubs through East. Again, it does not benefit him to ruff, so you win the ♣Q and now ruff the fourth round of clubs in dummy.

East can overruff or save his natural trump trick until later, but either way you will have twelve tricks and your contract.

This concept of leading through a potential ruff towards honors is an important one so let's take a look at a second example:

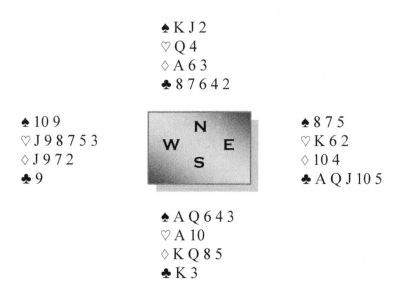

♠ K J 2
♡ Q 4
◊ A 6 3
♣ 8 7 6 4 2

♠ 10 9
♡ J 9 8 7 5 3
◊ J 9 7 2
♣ 9

♠ 8 7 5
♡ K 6 2
◊ 10 4
♣ A Q J 10 5

♠ A Q 6 4 3
♡ A 10
◊ K Q 8 5
♣ K 3

West leads the ♣9 against your Four Spades. East wins with the ace and returns a club to your king, ruffed by West with the ♠9. West then exits with the ♠10. You win in hand with the ace and play a second round of trumps to dummy's king, West discarding a heart.

You seem to have a potential loser in each red suit. Can you see a way of avoiding one of them?

If the diamonds split 3-3, you will be okay, but if they do not you will need to ruff your losing diamond in dummy. There will be no problem if East (the defender with the outstanding trump) has four diamonds, but what if he holds a doubleton?

You are not worried about the fourth round of diamonds getting overruffed as dummy's last trump, the jack, is higher than the last trump held by the defense. The problem is how to cash your three diamond winners without getting one of those ruffed.

The solution is to lead the third round of diamonds through the defender with the outstanding trump, East. Cash the king of diamonds and then cross to dummy's ace. When you then lead the third round of diamonds from dummy, what can East do?

If he discards, you will win with the ◊Q and ruff your diamond loser with the ♠J. You can then get back to your hand, draw East's last trump, and claim your contract, just losing a heart at the end.

If East ruffs in on the third round of diamonds, that will be the defenders' last trick. You will win the return, cash the ◊Q discarding a heart from dummy, and ruff your heart loser with the ♠J. Either way, you will make ten tricks.

Sometimes the opening lead sets up a potential ruff for the defense:

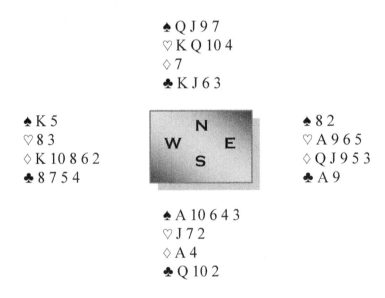

       ♠ Q J 9 7
       ♡ K Q 10 4
       ◊ 7
       ♣ K J 6 3

♠ K 5   ♠ 8 2
♡ 8 3   ♡ A 9 6 5
◊ K 10 8 6 2   ◊ Q J 9 5 3
♣ 8 7 5 4   ♣ A 9

       ♠ A 10 6 4 3
       ♡ J 7 2
       ◊ A 4
       ♣ Q 10 2

You reach Four Spades and West leads the ♡8. East wins the ace of hearts and returns the ♡5. How do you play?

The big decision on this deal is whether to take the trump finesse. With the ace of clubs a certain trick for the defense, you can afford to lose one trump trick but not two. Chances are high that one of the defenders has no more hearts, although you cannot be certain which.

If you take a losing trump finesse, the defenders will score a heart ruff to beat your contract if East began with a doubleton heart and at least two trumps. You will also go down if West has the short hearts and a second trump, and East can get in with the ace of clubs.

To give yourself the best chance of stopping the defenders from ruffing one of your winners, you need to draw trumps as quickly as possible. The odds heavily favor eschewing the finesse and, instead, playing a trump to the ace and then an immediate second round.

There are no 100% guarantees: East might hold the trump king and at least two low trumps along with the doubleton heart, with West holding the ace of clubs as an entry. In that scenario, taking the trump finesse is the winning line of play, but the odds are heavily against coming up against that precise layout of the defensive cards.

Sometimes you cannot draw all of the trumps before giving up the lead. Cover the E/W cards and decide how you would play this slam:

♠ Q 2
♡ A Q J
◇ Q 10 3
♣ K J 10 5 2

♠ K 10 7 5 3
♡ 9 7 4 3 2
◇ 7 6
♣ 3

♠ J 9 8 6
♡ 10 8 6 5
◇ A
♣ 9 8 6 4

♠ A 4
♡ K
◇ K J 9 8 5 4 2
♣ A Q 7

West leads the ♣3 against your Six Diamonds. How do you play?

Holding eight cards in the side suit led, you should be aware that the lead is probably a singleton. That the lead is also the lowest missing spot card reinforces the warning. With so many top tricks, surely you should lead trumps as quickly as possible, shouldn't you?

Sure, West may hold the ace of trumps, or he might hold singletons in both minors. As the cards lie, though, if you play a trump at trick two, East will win with the ace and play a club for his partner to ruff: not an unlikely scenario. A better option is to win the club lead and immediately play the ♡K, overtaking with dummy's ace. You can then cash the queen-jack of hearts, discarding clubs from your hand.

When you then play a trump, East wins and returns a club but you can ruff with a high trump. Re-entering dummy whilst drawing the last trump in the process then allows you to dispose of your spade loser on one of dummy's club winners.

On our next deal, the defense immediately threatens a winner:

None Vul: Dealer South

                ♠ K 9 7 2
                ♡ K J 4
                ◇ J 10 8 6 3
                ♣ 7

♠ A Q J 10 5 3   ♠ 8
♡ 9 3   ♡ Q 10 8 6 5
◇ 7   ◇ 9 4
♣ J 9 6 2   ♣ K Q 8 5 4

                ♠ 6 4
                ♡ A 7 2
                ◇ A K Q 5 2
                ♣ A 10 3

West	North	East	South
—	—	—	1◇
2♠	3◇	Dble	Redble
4♣	5◇	All Pass	

Three Notrumps would have been okay on a spade lead, but the opponents denied you the choice of taking that gamble. Against your Five Diamonds, West kicks off with the ♠A and continues with the queen of spades at trick two. How do you plan to make eleven tricks?

With the ace of spades onside, you seem to have only two losers, one in each major. What you would like to do, of course, is to draw trumps before the defenders endanger any of your high-card winners. However, West's aggressive opening salvo has immediately placed dummy's ♠K at the mercy of East's small trumps. What can be done?

I'd be willing to bet that if this deal was played in Five Diamonds at a large number of tables, what would happen at many of them would be: West leads the ace of spades; West continues with the ♠Q and East ruffs dummy's king; East returns the ♣K to declarer's ace; declarer now stops to think about how to play.

After this start, declarer will draw trumps and eventually take a heart finesse. When East shows up with the ♡Q, declarer will be one down. Many declarers will shrug their shoulders and bemoan their bad luck: "spades split 6-1 and the heart finesse failed so there was nothing I could do."

It was too late for declarer to start thinking after he had won trick three with the ♣A. As usual, declarer should have made a plan before playing to trick one or, in this case, at least before calling for dummy's ♠K at trick two.

It is not possible to make this contract if you allow East to ruff away one of your eleven winners (ie. the king of spades). Instead, you must allow West to win trick two with the ♠Q. Suppose he then continues with a third round of spades: you again play low from dummy and ruff this trick in your hand. You can then draw the defenders' trumps and eventually throw your heart loser on that carefully-preserved king of spades: eleven tricks.

Rather than losing one spade, one ruff and one heart, you lose only two spade tricks. This is not a difficult hand provided you stop to make a plan. Unfortunately, at the table there will be no kindly author sitting on your shoulder telling you that this is the time to stop and think before playing. That is a habit you simply have to get into.

The theme is similar on the next deal:

♠ J 9 4 3
♡ K 8
◇ A 8 6 3
♣ K J 4

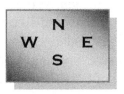

♠ A 10 7 2
♡ A 6 3
◇ K 7 5 2
♣ Q 3

You play in Four Spades and West leads the ◇4, which is likely to be a singleton.

How would you play?

You have six possible losers: two in spades, two in diamonds and one in each of the other suits. At least three of these are unavoidable: a trump, a diamond and the ace of clubs. You hope to limit your trump losses to one by taking two finesses in the suit, and the third heart can be ruffed in dummy. A 3-2 diamond break would take care of the second loser in that suit, but even a 4-1 split can be overcome as dummy's clubs can be established for a discard.

You must assume that East will hold at least one spade honor. You may therefore need to lead trumps twice from dummy. What other dangers does this deal present?

We mentioned above that you could overcome a 4-1 diamond break by discarding the fourth diamond from your hand on dummy's third club winner. If one of the defenders holds a singleton diamond, though, is there not also a chance that they may be able to score a diamond ruff?

You cannot afford to play the ace of trumps on the first round, so it is guaranteed that you will lose the lead whilst enemy trumps are still at large. What this means is that there is no way that you can prevent the defenders from ruffing a diamond. What you must arrange, though, is that when they do take a ruff they are only ruffing your losing diamond.

Analysis of the opening lead should lead you to the right answer: ask yourself "from what 4-card holding would West lead the ◊4?"

West would surely have led an honor from any of the possible 4-card combinations. Logic therefore suggests that if anyone holds a singleton it will be West. If that is the case, how will you make your contact?

The full hand will look something like this:

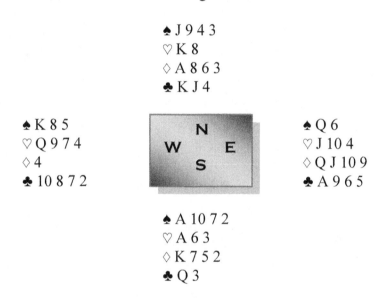

♠ J 9 4 3
♡ K 8
◊ A 8 6 3
♣ K J 4

♠ K 8 5
♡ Q 9 7 4
◊ 4
♣ 10 8 7 2

♠ Q 6
♡ J 10 4
◊ Q J 10 9
♣ A 9 6 5

♠ A 10 7 2
♡ A 6 3
◊ K 7 5 2
♣ Q 3

Suppose that because you want to be in dummy to lead trumps you win the opening lead with dummy's ◊A. You continue with a trump finesse taken by West with the ♠K. A club to East's ace is followed by the ◊Q. You cover with the king and West ruffs. (If you don't cover, East simply continues leading diamonds until you do.) You can win the club return with dummy's king, pick up the remaining trumps, discard one diamond on dummy's club winner, and ruff your heart loser, but you will still have a losing diamond at the end: one down.

You cannot prevent West ruffing a diamond, but you can make sure that he cannot do so profitably. Win the opening lead in hand with the ◊K and then cross to dummy with the ♡K to take a trump finesse. West wins and leads a club to East's ace, and again East returns the

◊Q. Does it help West to ruff this trick, though? Effectively, all he will be doing is ruffing his partner's diamond trick. Whether West ruffs or not makes no difference: you will lose either a diamond ruff or a later diamond trick to go with the ♠K and ♣A, but that is still only three losers. Contract made.

On the lead of the ◊4, you could be fairly sure that it would be West (if anyone) who held a singleton diamond. The same would be true if the lead was the ◊9. What about on the lead of the ◊Q, though?

A singleton queen is not a particularly attractive choice of opening lead as it will often cost a trick, but that does not mean you can rule out the possibility. On balance, though, the ◊Q lead is more likely to be from Q-J-10-9 or Q-J-10-4 or Q-J-9-4, leaving East with the singleton.

Now the full deal is more likely to look something like this:

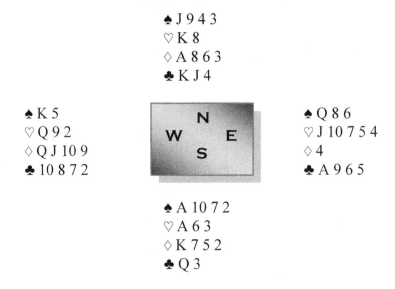

```
                    ♠ J 9 4 3
                    ♡ K 8
                    ◊ A 8 6 3
                    ♣ K J 4
  ♠ K 5                 N              ♠ Q 8 6
  ♡ Q 9 2           W       E          ♡ J 10 7 5 4
  ◊ Q J 10 9            S              ◊ 4
  ♣ 10 8 7 2                           ♣ A 9 6 5
                    ♠ A 10 7 2
                    ♡ A 6 3
                    ◊ K 7 5 2
                    ♣ Q 3
```

As before, it is imperative that you win trick one with the diamond honor that sits in front of the singleton: this time, dummy's ace. Your first trump finesse loses to West's king and he continues with the ◊J. Now it is East who can ruff, but at no gain for the defense. (Yes, you will still go down if West has the ♣A and East has three trumps as he can then get two diamond ruffs, but in that case the contract was always destined to fail.)

If the opening lead is either the ◊J or the ◊10, it is much more of a guess. The jack could be a singleton or from J-10-9-4 and the ten could be a singleton or from Q-10-9-4. Frankly, either defender could be the one with the singleton. You might base your decision on such inferences as 'How quickly did West lead the ◊10'? He might have though a while before leading from Q-10-9-4 perhaps, but led a singleton ten more quickly. Nothing is guaranteed, but you are ahead of the game if you at least know the reason for deciding where to win trick one.

Pre-emptive bidding by an opponent should always alert declarer to the possibility of bad breaks. With that clue, see if you can spot how to bring home your game on this next deal:

E/W Game: Dealer South

♠ K 6
♡ 9 4 2
◊ Q 2
♣ K 10 7 6 5 2

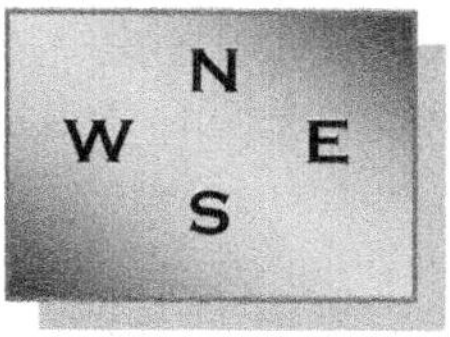

♠ A 9 5 3 2
♡ —
◊ A K J 10 9 5
♣ A 3

West	North	East	South
—	—	—	1◊
4♡	Pass	Pass	4♠
Pass	5◊	All Pass	

West leads the ♡K against your minor-suit game. How do you go about scoring eleven tricks?

When the deal occurred at the table, declarer correctly followed the principle of setting about the side suit first with a two-suited hand. He ruffed the opening lead and immediately played a spade to the king and a second spade back to the ace.

Unfortunately, West ruffed and exited with a trump. Declarer could ruff a spade with the ◊Q but that left him with only ten tricks: one down.

This declarer committed the cardinal sin of failing to count his tricks. Let's count them now and see what we come up with: six trumps in hand, one spade ruff in dummy, and two black-suit ace-kings seem to add up to eleven. Of course, declarer ended up one trick short because he made only one of his high spades rather than scoring both of them.

So, how should declarer have played?

This is another of those hands that require you to think 'outside the box', to use a modern expression. In other words, to NOT do what comes naturally,

Having ruffed the opening lead in hand and played a spade to the king successfully, declarer was just about home. Can you see what he should have done next?

Declarer was right to continue with a second round of spades. His error was to expose the ace to a potential ruff. Notice what happens if you follow with a low spade from your hand on this trick.

No matter what the defense does now, you will be able to ruff a spade with the ◊Q, draw trumps, and score the ♠A later along with your top clubs.

I'm sure that you are a fine upstanding citizen. No matter how virtuous you may be, the Bridge Gods will still occasionally give the enemy sufficient tricks to defeat your contract. So far as I know, though, there is nothing in the laws of the game that decrees you must simply sit there like a bump on a log and accept their decision?

What do you think of your chances on the following deal?

N/S Game: Dealer West

♠ J 9 4 3
♡ J 8 3
♢ Q 6 3
♣ 8 6 4

♠ 5
♡ A Q 10 9 7 4 2
♢ 9 8
♣ Q 9 7

```
      N
  W       E
      S
```

♠ 8 6
♡ 6
♢ K J 10 7 4 2
♣ J 10 5 2

♠ A K Q 10 7 2
♡ K 5
♢ A 5
♣ A K 3

West	North	East	South
4♡	Pass	Pass	4♠
All Pass			

West leads the ♡A and continues hearts at trick two, East ruffing away your king. You win the club return and draw trumps.

Perhaps you now lead ace and another diamond, hoping to find the king onside and thus establishing the ♢Q for a club discard. Maybe you run your trumps, hoping to endplay East at the end with the third round of clubs to force him to lead away from the ♢K. Whichever option you go for, it does not work. Unlucky – West found the winning opening lead, the ♢K was wrong, West held Q-x-x clubs. There was nothing you could have done. Or was there?

Can you see how you might have made this contract?

It is sometimes useful to mentally move around the table, to sit in a defender's seat, and look at things from his perspective. On this deal, take the West cards and ask yourself how you would defend after the first trick has gone ♡A, ♡3, ♡6, ♡K.

Can you honestly put your hand on heart and swear that you would continue hearts now?

Suppose that instead West switches to a diamond at trick two. You

103

can try dummy's queen, but East covers and you win with the ace. Now you can draw trumps and surprise West by leading your carefully concealed ♡5 towards dummy's jack, establishing a parking place for your club loser. Voila! All of a sudden, nine tricks have become ten.

The deal above offers a spectacular example of deflecting a ruff by feigning shortness in the suit, but there are more mundane situations in which similar methods can be used. Take a look at this suit layout:

♣ Q 8 7 3

♣ A K 10 6 5  ♣ 2

♣ J 9 4

Suppose West leads a high club against your Four Spade contract. You can afford to lose two club tricks, but not a ruff as well. Your best chance is to follow with the ♣J from your hand at trick one.

This will not always work, or course – for a start, the bidding may have precluded you from holding a singleton. The success of this type of deceptive card is also dependent on what signaling method E/W employ. If E/W play standard count signals, then East's ♣2 would be the normal card from 9-4-2. If you are unlucky and East's singleton happens to be the ♣9, you will never persuade good defenders that you ♣J is singleton, unless of course they are playing reverse count signals (when the ♣9 would be consistent with 9-4-2).

If you are desperate, though, nothing is lost by trying. The worst that can happen is that the defenders will take the ruff they were due anyway.

Quiz Hands

1.

♠ A 4
♡ 10 9 6 5
◇ A 8 5
♣ K J 6 3

♠ Q J 10
♡ A Q J 7 3
◇ Q J 10 7 4
♣ —

You bid to Four Hearts after West has overcalled in clubs.
West leads the ◇2. How do you play?

2.

♠ 9 7 2
♡ Q 10 9 7 6 4 2
◇ A
♣ Q 4

♠ K 10 4
♡ K J 5
◇ K J 7 2
♣ A J 3

East opens 1◇ and you overcall 1NT. After a transfer, you declare
Four Hearts as South. West leads the ◇9. How do you play?

105

1.

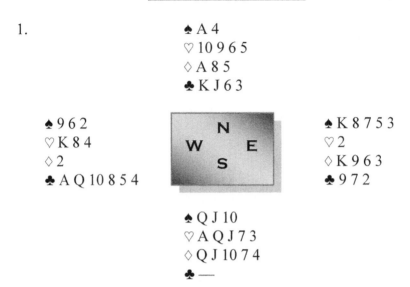

              ♠ A 4
              ♡ 10 9 6 5
              ◊ A 8 5
              ♣ K J 6 3

♠ 9 6 2　　　　　　　　　　　　　♠ K 8 7 5 3
♡ K 8 4　　　　　　　　　　　　　♡ 2
◊ 2　　　　　　　　　　　　　　　◊ K 9 6 3
♣ A Q 10 8 5 4　　　　　　　　　♣ 9 7 2

              ♠ Q J 10
              ♡ A Q J 7 3
              ◊ Q J 10 7 4
              ♣ —

You bid to Four Hearts after West has overcalled in clubs. West leads the ◊2.

Finesses are wonderful things – everyone loves to make a cheap trick. With finesses available in three suits on this deal, how many do you think you should take?

The first decision is whether to take the diamond finesse at trick one. West's 2-level overcall suggests that he will hold most of the defenders' high cards, after all.

When a defender bids a suit and then leads a different one, you should always be on high alert for a short-suit lead, particularly when you hold eight or more cards in the suit led. The lead of the deuce is also a warning of a possible singleton. You should rise with the ◊A and start on trumps immediately. Should you now take the trump finesse?

Doing so poses an unnecessary risk – suppose West's diamond lead was from K-x-x-x. If you take a losing trump finesse to West's king, he will then be able to cash the ◊K and give his partner a diamond ruff. By playing trumps from the top, you eliminate this chance: by the time a defender gains the lead with the ♡K, his partner will have no trumps left.

Both defenders follow to the ace of trumps. West wins the second round of trumps with the king as East discards a club. West now switches to the ♠2. Having already turned down finesses in two suits, are you now tempted in the third?

You can afford to lose a spade trick, What you cannot afford is for East to win with the ♠K and give his partner a diamond ruff with the last outstanding trump. Win with the ♠A, draw the last trump, and then knock out the ◊K. The ♠K is the third trick for the defense, but that is their lot.

It was correct to refuse all three potential finesses on this deal. As it happens, your contract would have survived if you had taken only the trump finesse, but there were layouts of the defensive cards where that would also have been disastrous.

2.

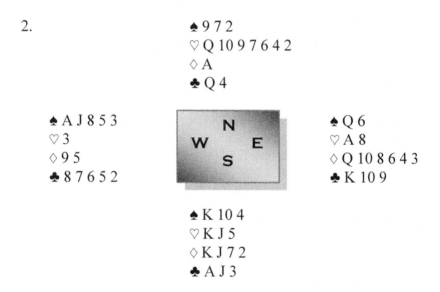

```
                    ♠ 9 7 2
                    ♡ Q 10 9 7 6 4 2
                    ◊ A
                    ♣ Q 4

♠ A J 8 5 3              N              ♠ Q 6
♡ 3              W              E       ♡ A 8
◊ 9 5                   S              ◊ Q 10 8 6 4 3
♣ 8 7 6 5 2                            ♣ K 10 9

                    ♠ K 10 4
                    ♡ K J 5
                    ◊ K J 7 2
                    ♣ A J 3
```

East opens One Diamond and you overcall 1NT. After a transfer sequence, you declare Four Hearts and West leads the ◊9. All looks rosy in declarer's garden, and it is on such occasions that you must be particularly vigilant. Ask yourself, "What can go wrong?"

When this deal occurred in a knock-out match, declarer at the first table failed to ask this question but was quickly provided with the answer by the defenders. He won the ◊A and immediately led a trump from dummy. East hopped up with the ♡A and switched to the ♠Q.

107

Whether declarer covered this or not mattered little: the defenders were destined to take either three spade tricks or two spade tricks and a ruff to beat the contract.

Yes, the layout of the spade suit was unfortunate, particularly after East's opening bid, but that is no excuse. Spotting how you might spike Lady Luck's guns when she is on her worst behavior is a primary difference between winning and losing players.

When the deal was replayed at the second table, declarer realized that the primary source of potential danger was the spade suit. Rather than play a trump at trick two, he instead advanced the ♣Q. As expected, East covered with the ♣K and declarer won with the ace. In hand now, declarer quickly played the ◇K and, when West had to follow suit, dummy's third spade as discarded. Now, when declarer played a trump, the defenders were powerless since dummy had plenty of high trumps to deal with a third round of spades.

Note that if East does not cover the ♣Q, declarer can safely finesse. Even if the finesse loses, there is no suit in which West might make a threatening return. (If West turns up with the ♣K, the ♠A is sure to be onside.)

This deal illustrates the importance of counting your potential losers, something you should do before playing to trick one every time you play a suit contract. Counting your losers and coming up with a plan for reducing them to the required number will often provide an answer to the question of when to draw trumps.

Chapter 7 – Playing the Trump Suit

So far we have concentrated primarily on the question of when to draw trumps. Often it will be *how* trumps are drawn that is the key to success.

It is important that you learn the correct technical way to play a number of common suit combinations (or at least understand how to work out the best play). In this chapter, we will examine some suit combinations that you would be pleased to have as your trump suit. Take a look at these two layouts:

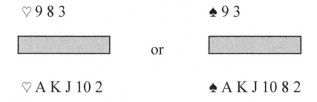

How would you play each of these combinations to give yourself the maximum chance of avoiding a loser in the suit?

In each case, you hold eight trumps between your hand and dummy. If the missing cards in the suit break 3-2, the odds are 60:40 (3-to-2) that the queen will be held by the defender with the three-card holding. If West has Q-x-x you cannot avoid losing a trick and if East holds Q-x you cannot go wrong, so the key position occurs when West holds a doubleton.

Playing off the ace and king hoping to drop the queen will work 40% of the time, but taking the finesse will be right 60%. Finessing against the queen, therefore, offers the best chance to avoid losing a trick in the suit. Exactly when should you take that finesse, though?

So far we have only considered the cases where the missing cards in the suit split 3-2. What about when one of the defenders holds a singleton? Once again, you can disregard the cases where East is short in the suit (since all plays lead to the same result). What about when West holds a singleton?

Let's look at a full deal where the heart suit above is trumps:

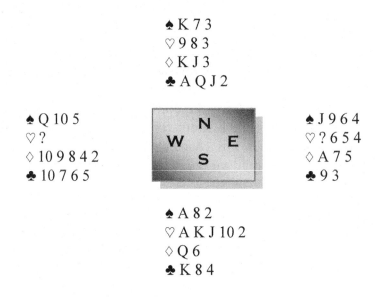

```
              ♠ K 7 3
              ♡ 9 8 3
              ◇ K J 3
              ♣ A Q J 2

  ♠ Q 10 5          N          ♠ J 9 6 4
  ♡ ?          W         E     ♡ ? 6 5 4
  ◇ 10 9 8 4 2       S         ◇ A 7 5
  ♣ 10 7 6 5                   ♣ 9 3

              ♠ A 8 2
              ♡ A K J 10 2
              ◇ Q 6
              ♣ K 8 4
```

You reach Six Hearts and West leads the ◇10. East wins with the ace of diamonds and returns the suit. How should you play?

We have established that taking a finesse offers better odds than playing off the ace and king hoping that the queen comes down. Does this mean, though, that you should win the diamond return in dummy and immediately take a heart finesse?

Would it not be irritating in the extreme if your finesse lost and it subsequently transpired that West's ♡Q was singleton?

There is no need to take that particular risk. With a 5-3 trump fit, you can afford to cash one high honor before taking the finesse.

The '?' in the East and West hands in the diagram above represent the ♡Q and the ♡7. If the queen is singleton in the West hand, it will fall when you cash the ♡A at trick three and your problems will be over. Suppose instead that West follows with the ♡7, you can then cross to dummy with the ♠K and lead the ♡9. If East does not cover, you intend to run the nine, finessing against East's presumed queen. When West discards on this trick, you will be able to play a third round of trumps from dummy and repeat the finesse.

Having drawn East's fourth trump you can discard your losing spade on one of dummy's minor-suit winners and claim your slam.

The trump suit on the next deal looks similar, so does that mean it should be played in the same way? How should you play to give yourself the best chance of landing this slam contract?

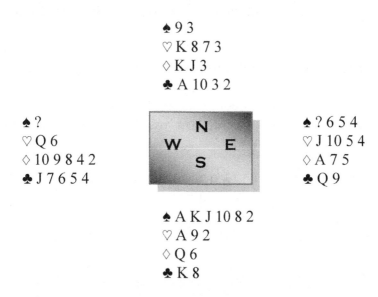

♠ 9 3
♡ K 8 7 3
◇ K J 3
♣ A 10 3 2

♠ ?
♡ Q 6
◇ 10 9 8 4 2
♣ J 7 6 5 4

♠ ? 6 5 4
♡ J 10 5 4
◇ A 7 5
♣ Q 9

♠ A K J 10 8 2
♡ A 9 2
◇ Q 6
♣ K 8

Declarer in the final of one of the USA's major team events was faced with playing this deal in Six Spades and, when he went down, it cost his team the trophy. He played the spades in the way described above as correct when the fit is 5-3. Can you spot why a different approach is needed when you play in a 6-2 fit?

As before, I have replaced both the Queen and the seven of the key suit with question marks in the diagram.

Again, the defense begins with a diamond to the ace and a second round of that suit. How should you play this time?

If you start by cashing one top spade honor (which is what the player mentioned above did), you may fell a singleton queen in the West hand. When West holds a singleton spade, though, it is four times more likely to be a low one than the queen. Can you see what happens if, having cashed one high honor, you then finesse successfully on the second round but West discards?

East will then be left with a guarded ♠Q but you will have no trump left in dummy to repeat the finesse. You will make your slam on the 20% of hands (1-in-5) when West's singleton is the queen, but you will have to lose a trump trick on the 80% when West's singleton is a low card.

Playing in a 6-2 fit, the best percentage play is to lead dummy's nine on the first round of spades, and run it if East does not cover. If the nine wins, you will then be able to repeat the finesse on the second round, and still score six tricks in the suit even if East started with four trumps to the queen.

Before we leave this suit combination, let's see one more deal with this spade suit as trumps. Decide how you would play before reading on, and remember to think!

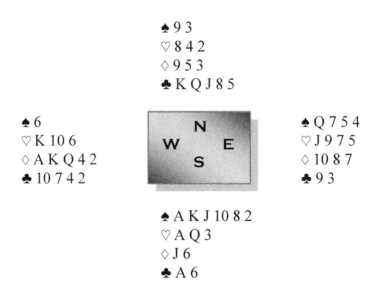

                    ♠ 9 3
                    ♡ 8 4 2
                    ◇ 9 5 3
                    ♣ K Q J 8 5

  ♠ 6   ♠ Q 7 5 4
  ♡ K 10 6   N   ♡ J 9 7 5
  ◇ A K Q 4 2   W   E   ◇ 10 8 7
  ♣ 10 7 4 2   S   ♣ 9 3

                    ♠ A K J 10 8 2
                    ♡ A Q 3
                    ◇ J 6
                    ♣ A 6

You quickly reach Four Spades, and West kicks off the defense by leading three top diamonds. Having ruffed the third round of diamonds, how do you continue?

We know how to play this spade suit to give ourselves the maximum chance of avoiding a trump loser – we lead the ♠9 from dummy and run it if East does not play the queen. When the nine holds, we can then repeat the finesse, and in so doing neutralize East's queen.

However, the optimal play in a single suit is not always the best play in the context of a complete deal. Here, even though East holds four trumps to the queen, taking this winning finesse will cost you your contract.

When you think about the complete deal, you should see why: ask yourself how you plan on getting to dummy to take the trump finesse? The only route to dummy is in clubs. Suppose you cross to dummy and take the winning spade finesses. After drawing trumps, you will be stuck in your hand, left with two heart losers and nowhere to put them.

Instead, you should ruff the third round of diamonds and immediately play off the ace and king of spades. The ♠Q does not fall, but you can force it out now.

East returns a heart – are you going to finesse?

Of course not. Win with the ♡A, remember to draw East's last trump, and then safely cash dummy's club winners to throw your losing hearts away.

Here is another common trump suit layout:

♡ 7 6 4 3   ♡ K 7 3

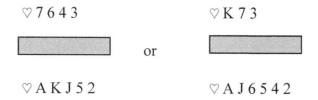   or

♡ A K J 5 2   ♡ A J 6 5 4 2

You again have a suit with the queen of trumps missing. This time, though, instead of eight trumps you have nine. Note that the two heart layouts diagrammed above may look different but, in terms of how to play to give yourself the best chance of avoiding a loser in the suit, they are the same. Whether you are in a 5-4 fit, a 6-3 fit, or even a 7-2 fit, and whether the high honors are together or split makes no difference.

There are essentially two ways you might choose to play suits that look something like those diagrammed above. One option is to simply lay down the top two honors hoping to drop the queen. The alternative is to cash one high honor and (assuming both defenders follow suit) then lead towards your ace-jack or king-jack combination intending to finesse against the queen.

Taking these 9-card combinations missing the queen in isolation, the odds marginally favor playing for the drop rather than taking the finesse. Essentially, the player sitting over the jack is slightly more likely to hold the doubleton queen than a low singleton.

Let's look at a couple of full deals involving these 9-card combinations. We start with another slam deal:

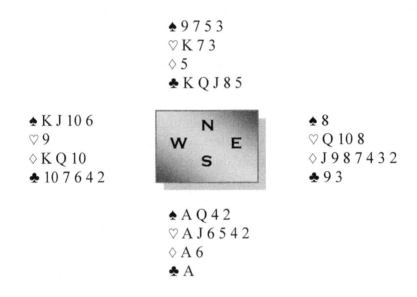

♠ 9 7 5 3
♡ K 7 3
◊ 5
♣ K Q J 8 5

♠ K J 10 6
♡ 9
◊ K Q 10
♣ 10 7 6 4 2

♠ 8
♡ Q 10 8
◊ J 9 8 7 4 3 2
♣ 9 3

♠ A Q 4 2
♡ A J 6 5 4 2
◊ A 6
♣ A

West leads the ◊K against your Six Heart contract.

How would you play?

You have quite a few potential losers for a slam contract: one diamond, one heart and three spades. Dummy's clubs will provide discards for some of those losers but you must be careful about using your entries wisely.

Note that this contract is 100% as long as neither defender holds all four missing trumps. What's more, you will still bring home your contract even if you lose a trick to the ♡Q.

You should win the opening diamond lead and immediately cash the ♡A. When both defenders follow, you have twelve tricks. (Try counting them before you read on.)

Unblock the ♣A and cross to dummy by playing a heart to the king. West discards but that does not matter. You now start leading dummy's winning clubs, discarding spades from your hand. East can ruff the third round of clubs with his trump winner and lead a spade, but your contract is safe. You rise with the ace of spades, enter dummy by ruffing your diamond, and throw your last spade loser on dummy's remaining club winner.

If this deal was played in a large field, I suspect that many players would fail in this slam because they would take an immediate diamond ruff at trick two. Play it through to see what happens if you do this – you will discover that you then have to guess very well to avoid losing both a heart and a spade.

Simply knowing how to play a specific suit combination is no substitute for thinking. Let us visit one more of these 9-card combinations before moving on:

♠ 6 4
♡ K 7 5 3
◇ K 8 6 2
♣ K 5 2

♠ A 7 5 2
♡ A J 6 4 2
◇ Q 4
♣ A 3

You bid unopposed to Four Hearts and West leads the ♠K. How would you play?

Start by counting losers: potentially, you have three spades, one heart and one diamond. You can do nothing about the ◇A and one of the spade losers, and you may or may not have to lose a trump. Your plan, therefore, should be to ruff the third and fourth round of spades in dummy.

Trying to take these ruffs before drawing trumps is fraught with danger. Having decided to draw trumps first, though, how should you do so?

We have already established that the optimal percentage play for no loser in the heart suit is to cash the ace and the king. If you adopt this approach and trumps split 2-2, you can now ruff your two spade losers in dummy and make eleven tricks.

Suppose instead, though, that West discards on the second round of trumps: you can then exit with a spade but East wins, cashes his ♡Q, and plays a third round of spades. You ruff with dummy's last trump and play a diamond to your queen. East wins and cashes a spade to put your contract one down.

That was unlucky – trumps didn't break. Or was it?

Actually, this contract is guaranteed once both defenders follow to the first round of trumps. Although playing the two top trumps is the best percentage play in hearts taking that suit in isolation, you should not be playing purely by rote. Instead, think about how to play the key suit in the context of the whole hand. We've already seen what can happen if you play off the two top trumps. Now think about the subsequent play if you finesse.

Suppose you take the second-round trump finesse and your ♡J loses to West's queen. How many tricks will you then make? With trumps breaking 2-2, dummy still has two trumps left to take care of both your third and fourth spade. You will lose the ◇A, the ♡Q and just one spade: ten tricks.

Now suppose that when you take the trump finesse West discards, so your ♡J wins. You can then draw East's last trump with the ♡A. There is now only one trump left in dummy so you can ruff only one of your three spade losers, but that's okay. You lose just the ◇A and two spades: ten tricks again.

Whilst playing the ace on the second round of hearts gives you the best chance of avoiding a trump loser, doing so also means that you will end up with either nine or eleven tricks.

Taking the second round finesse marginally increases your chance of losing a trump trick, but ensures also that you will make exactly ten tricks, irrespective of how the opposition's cards lie. Having bid to the 4-level, it is therefore 100% right to finesse on the second round of trumps. (Note that if you were playing this deal in Five Hearts for some reason, it would then be 100% correct to play for the drop in trumps.)

Note also that declarer should allow West to win trick one with the king of spades on this deal. To see why, notice what happens if you win the ♠A and immediately play a trump to the king and a second round intending to finesse but East shows out.

When you now concede the second round of spades, the defense will be able to cash their trump winner to remove one of dummy's trumps.

Our next suit combination appears to be even more robust:

♠ A 9 7 2

♠ K Q 10 5 4

Suppose you are playing a spade contract with this trump suit and you decide it is time to draw trumps. Your contract is safe provided you do not lose a trump trick, so which honor should you cash first?

There is no danger unless the defenders' trumps divide 4-0 so you should focus on how to overcome such a split. First, let's assume that East holds all four missing trumps: whether you start by cashing the ace first or an honor from your hand, you will be able to pick up East's jack via a finesse.

What if it is West who holds all four missing spades, though?

Now if you win the first round of trumps with dummy's ace and East discards, you will then have to lose a trick to West's jack. If you start with one of the honors from your hand, though, you will still be able to pick up the suit for no loser.

So, when you are missing four trumps to the jack you can make sure of picking the suit up for no loser by first cashing an honor from the hand with two high honors. Whichever defender holds all four missing trumps, you will see the bad break in time to take a winning finesse against his jack.

This next combination looks very similar, but can you see why the solution is quite different?

117

♠ A 9 7 2

♠ K Q 8 5 4

Again, start by asking yourself how you can pick the suit up for no loser if either defender holds all four missing trumps.

Suppose East holds ♠J-10-6-3. Let's first see what happens if, as before, we start by cashing one of the honors from our hand. When West discards, there is now no way to avoid losing a trick to East's remaining J-10-x. If, however, we start by cashing the ace first, we will still be able to pick up East's holding by leading twice towards our hand (assuming we have an outside entry to dummy).

What if it is West who holds all four missing trumps?

I'll leave you to experiment with various lines of play, but what you will discover is that when East is void you will have to lose a trump trick no matter what you do.

This is a fairly common situation that comes in a number of guises: when you try to work out how to play a particular suit combination, you will often discover that you can pick up a bad break if one defender is short but not the other.

As a beginner, we all learned to cash the honor in the short hand first to avoid a blockage. Here is another example where the correct play goes against basic principles:

♠ A 10 4

♠ K Q 7 6 3 2

It may look natural to start this suit by cashing the ace, but to do so would be wrong. Again, ask yourself what can be done if one defender holds all four missing trumps. Once you stop to think about it, you will realize that you can do nothing if East holds ♠J-9-8-5. He has a natural trump trick and that's all there is to it. However, if it is East who is void and West who has the four missing trumps, you can avoid a trump loser provided you discover the bad split in time: cash one of the top honors from your hand first. If East discards, you can then finesse dummy's ten on the second round of the suit, cash the ace, cross back to your hand in a side suit, and draw West's last trump with your remaining high honor.

Let's see a variation on this theme by putting this type of suit into a full deal:

♠ K 10 4
♡ A K 9 2
◇ A K
♣ 8 7 5 2

♠ A Q 7 6 3 2
♡ Q 4
◇ 9 2
♣ 10 6 3

You open a weak Two Spades as Dealer and your partner raises to game. West starts by cashing three top clubs, East following twice and then discarding a diamond. You are about to lean forward and claim the rest of the tricks, but before you can do so West plays a fourth round of clubs and East ruffs with the ♠8.

When the deal occurred in a recent teams match, one declarer made the contract because he continued thinking. The other went down through sheer carelessness. If nothing else, I hope that having stuck with me this far you will be the 'thinking declarer' next time you are in this type of position.

So, having overruffed the ♠8 with the queen, how should declarer now play?

Of course, once you stop to think, you will realize that there is a danger that one defender has all three remaining trumps. But which defender?

If you are unsure, go back to original layout discussed above. This is really exactly the same situation in a slightly disguised form. Once again, if West began with ♠J-9-5 he always had a trump trick and nothing has changed. You will still have to lose a trick to him.

What is vital is that you do not lose a trump trick if East's ♠8 is a singleton, which is exactly what you will do if you now play a spade to the king after overruffing. If you start by cashing the ace and West discards, then your contract will go down but then there was never anything you could do about that – East always had a trump trick and that's all there is to it. Unlucky!

If East shows out when you cash the ♠A, you can still pick up West's trumps by finessing the ten on the second round: +620 and a 12-IMP gain against the careless declarer at the other table.

How should you play the following common suit combination to give yourself the best chance of the maximum number of tricks?

♠ K 6 2

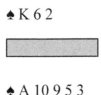

♠ A 10 9 5 3

If the defenders' spades split 3-2, any vaguely sensible way of playing this suit will produce four tricks and lose just one. The objective, therefore, is to cater for at least some of the 4-1 breaks too.

If West began with a holding such as ♠ Q-J-8-4 you can do nothing to avoid two losers in the suit. What, though if it is East with that sort of holding?

Cashing the ace give first gives up any chance of nullifying a 4-card holding in the East hand, so you win the first round of the suit with dummy's king. You then play a second round of trumps from dummy and, if East follows with the last remaining low spade, you can simply cover his card.

If West wins this trick with one of the missing honors, the suit will have broken evenly and the second missing honor will fall under your ace on the third round of the suit.

If, however, West began with a low singleton, your nine (or ten) will win the second round of the suit. Playing the ace and a fourth round then establishes your fifth card as a winner and, again, you will score four tricks in the suit for the loss of just one.

A little learning, though, can be a dangerous thing, so let us look at this suit in the context of a full deal. Cover the E/W cards and decide how you would play:

<u>N/S Game: Dealer West</u>

♠ K 6 2
♡ 8 2
◊ A K Q 4
♣ K J 8 6

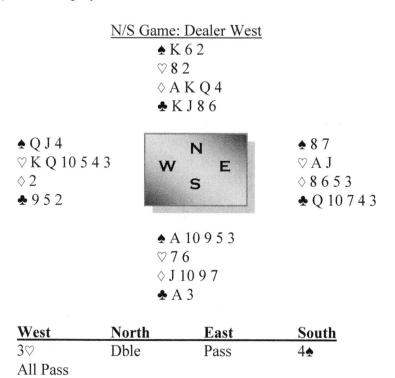

♠ Q J 4
♡ K Q 10 5 4 3
◊ 2
♣ 9 5 2

♠ 8 7
♡ A J
◊ 8 6 5 3
♣ Q 10 7 4 3

♠ A 10 9 5 3
♡ 7 6
◊ J 10 9 7
♣ A 3

West	North	East	South
3♡	Dble	Pass	4♠
All Pass			

West opens Three Hearts in first seat and your partner doubles for takeout. Your jump to Four Spades concludes the auction and West leads the ◊2.

How should you play?

This seems like a fairly straightforward deal: as long as you can avoid losing two trump tricks you will surely be okay. Luckily, you have learned how to safety-play this spade suit to give yourself the best chance of avoiding two losers. So, you duly win the opening diamond lead, play the ♠K and then lead a second round of trumps. East follows with the ♠8, so you cover with the nine.

You are about to claim your contract when things go horribly wrong: West wins the second spade with the jack, cashes the ♡K, plays a second heart to his partner's ace, and ruffs the second round of diamonds with the ♠Q. One down! That was unlucky, wasn't it?

Actually, there were numerous clues that should enable you to foresee this potential calamity, and thus avoid it.

Firstly, when an opponent makes a pre-emptive bid and then subsequently leads one of the other two side suits, the lead is very often a singleton. Think about it – West undoubtedly holds some strong combination of heart honors that would have provided him with an attractive-looking opening lead. Why, then, did he lead a diamond instead?

Suppose, however, that the bidding had been different and you had not been favored with West's pre-emptive opening bid. Even against silent opposition, you should be acutely aware of the danger of an impending ruff whenever an opponent makes an opening lead in a side suit where your side holds eight or more cards.

Having come to the conclusion that West's opening diamond lead is a singleton, you should not be tempted by the safety play in trumps. Yes, it is not impossible that West was dealt specifically a 1-7-1-4 shape, but even then he might not have led his singleton when holding only one trump.

Much more likely, is something like the layout shown in the diagram above. Draw trumps by laying down the ace and king on the first two rounds. If the suit divides 4-1, then that is just unlucky.

Note also that you are not necessarily finished even if West shows out on the second round of trumps. You can still take a club finesse and, if it wins, discard one of your heart losers to make your game for the loss of only two trumps and one heart.

As a final point on the deal above, how would you have played if your trump suit had instead been:

♠ K 6 2

▭

♠ A J 5 3 2

With this combination, of course, you would usually start by leading to the king and then finessing the jack on the second round. Put this suit into the hand above and, if West began with ♠Q-x-x, you would again go down in similar fashion when he scores two hearts and a diamond ruff after winning the second round of trumps with the queen.

To avoid this fate, you should instead play the trumps by cashing the ace and then leading a second round to dummy's king. Remember, you can afford to lose ONE trump trick. If East began with a holding such as Q-10-9-x you can still restrict him to one winner in the suit (the queen) by leading the third round of the suit towards your jack.

Quiz Hands

1.

None Vul: Dealer West

♠ 10 7 6 3
♥ 10 5 4
♦ 8 6 3
♣ Q 7 2

♠ 9 4
♥ A 8
♦ A Q 10 9 4 2
♣ A K 5

West	North	East	South
1♥	Pass	1♠	3♦
All Pass			

West opens with the ♥K against your diamond partial
How should you play?

124

2.

♠ J 9 5 4
♡ 10 3
◊ 8 5 3
♣ A 7 5 3

♠ A Q 10 3
♡ 7 4
◊ A K 2
♣ K Q J 2

You reach Four Spades.
West leads the ♡K and a second heart to his partner's ace.
East then switches to the ♣8.
How do you play?

1.

<u>None Vul: Dealer West</u>

♠ 10 7 6 3
♡ 10 5 4
◇ 8 6 3
♣ Q 7 2

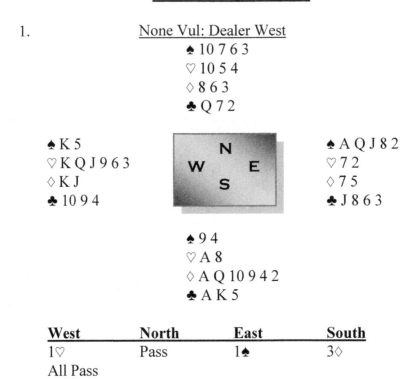

♠ K 5
♡ K Q J 9 6 3
◇ K J
♣ 10 9 4

♠ A Q J 8 2
♡ 7 2
◇ 7 5
♣ J 8 6 3

♠ 9 4
♡ A 8
◇ A Q 10 9 4 2
♣ A K 5

West	North	East	South
1♡	Pass	1♠	3◇
All Pass			

West leads the ♡K. You have three losers in the major suits (one heart and two spades) so you just need to avoid losing two trump tricks. How will you play the trump suit?

One option is to take the ♡A, enter dummy with the ♣Q, and lead a diamond to the queen.

After winning with the ◇K, West cashes his heart winner and then plays the king of spades and a second spade to his partner's ace. When East then continues with a third round of spades, you ruff with ◇10 but West overruffs with the jack and your contract is one down.

You can afford to lose one trump trick, but not two. A better approach is to start drawing trumps as quickly as possible: win with the ace of hearts at trick one and immediately lay down the ace of trumps.

This will bring immediate joy if West happens to have been dealt the singleton king. On the actual layout West drops the jack under the ace and East follows with the four, so you can now simply continue with the ◇Q to drive out the king.

Had both defenders followed with low trumps on the first round, you would have crossed to the queen of clubs to lead the second round of trumps from dummy in case East began with ◇K-J-x.

2.

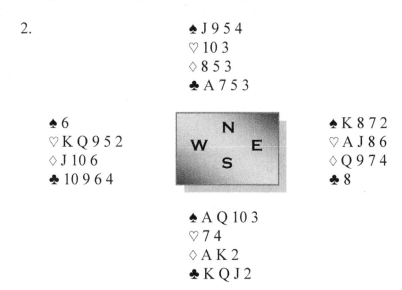

♠ J 9 5 4
♡ 10 3
◇ 8 5 3
♣ A 7 5 3

♠ 6
♡ K Q 9 5 2
◇ J 10 6
♣ 10 9 6 4

♠ K 8 7 2
♡ A J 8 6
◇ Q 9 7 4
♣ 8

♠ A Q 10 3
♡ 7 4
◇ A K 2
♣ K Q J 2

Against your Four Spade contract, the defense kicks off with the king of hearts, a heart to East's ace, and a club switch.

You have an unavoidable diamond loser so the success of your contract depends on avoiding a trump loser. Any reasonable line of play will work if East holds the ♠K and only two or three trumps. What if he holds four trumps, though?

This is a suit combination that you might not have seen before. The problem is how to take the trump finesse three times with only one entry to dummy.

If you start trumps by leading low from dummy and finessing, you will be stuck in hand and will then have to concede a trick to East's king even if he has only three trumps.

You can take the trump finesse twice by starting with the jack. Which card will you play from your hand, though? If you follow with the ♠3 then you will be forced to win the second round of trumps in hand. If, instead, you unblock the ♠10, East will then be able to take a trick by force (by covering with the king if you lead the nine next).

In order to take the trump finesse three times, you must start by leading the ♠9. You can then lead the jack from dummy on the second round of trumps (under-playing with the ten from your hand). This leaves you conveniently in dummy to take a third finesse and pick up a 4-card trump holding in the East hand.

Chapter 8 – Discovering How to Play Trumps

In the previous chapter, we looked at some common trump suit combinations and saw how to play them for the maximum number of tricks. We also considered how to vary the play in an individual suit to match the requirements of the deal as a whole. We continue in similar vein here with a look at how other factors might affect your play in the trump suit.

Our trump suit on this deal is a familiar one:

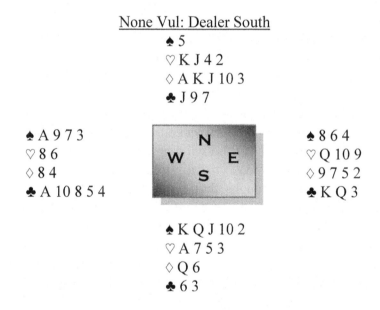

None Vul: Dealer South

```
               ♠ 5
               ♡ K J 4 2
               ◇ A K J 10 3
               ♣ J 9 7

♠ A 9 7 3              N              ♠ 8 6 4
♡ 8 6          W              E       ♡ Q 10 9
◇ 8 4                 S              ◇ 9 7 5 2
♣ A 10 8 5 4                         ♣ K Q 3

               ♠ K Q J 10 2
               ♡ A 7 5 3
               ◇ Q 6
               ♣ 6 3
```

West	North	East	South
—	—	—	1♠
Pass	2◇	Pass	2♡
Pass	4♡	All Pass	

Fortunately, West does not lead the unbid suit against your Four Heart contract, choosing instead the ♡8. How would you play?

129

With three top losers in the black suits, you theoretically need to avoid losing a trump trick in order to make your contract. If you took this heart suit on its own, the normal way to play would be to cash the ace and then finesse against the queen on the second round. Indeed, had the defenders taken their three winners before relinquishing the lead, this is precisely how you should play. Surely, though, the opening trump lead strongly suggests that the ♡Q will be in the East hand. So, what can be done?

Perhaps you can throw your club losers on dummy's diamonds? When the deal occurred at the table, declarer won the opening lead with the ♡A and immediately started on diamonds. He pitched a club loser on the third round of diamonds, but West ruffed and cashed his two aces. With East still holding the guarded queen of trumps, the contract was soon one down.

To prevent this happening, you must draw a second round of trumps (no finesses!) before starting diamonds. Who knows, perhaps East's queen of hearts will even fall under the king. It doesn't this time, but that is still okay as long as the defender with the winning trump also holds at least two diamonds. As it happens, East has to follow to enough diamonds that you can dispose of both club losers. You lose only the ♠A and ♡Q and wind up with eleven tricks.

West's opening trump lead virtually told you that the trump finesse would fail. Suppose, though, that he had instead led a diamond. Should you then put all of your eggs into the trump finesse basket?

Taking the finesse gives you only a 50% chance. However, playing off the two top trumps and then cashing diamonds offers much better odds of success. This line of play fails when taking the trump finesse would have worked only when West holds any four trumps including the queen or Q-x-x AND a singleton diamond.

One of the toughest tasks for bridge teachers is to get inexperienced players to take finesses – "…but I can win this trick and if I finesse I might lose it…" Then, once the penny drops and the concept of scoring cheap tricks sinks in, comes the even more difficult task of learning when NOT to take finesses.

Let's have a look at another deal with a similar trump suit:

```
                        ♠ K 5
                        ♡ K J 4 2
                        ◊ A K 2
                        ♣ A 9 7 3
  ♠ Q J 9 7 4 3                              ♠ 8
  ♡ 8 5            ┌──────────────┐          ♡ Q 9 6
  ◊ 8 4 3         │      N       │          ◊ J 9 7 5
  ♣ J 5           │  W       E   │          ♣ Q 10 8 6 4
                   │      S       │
                   └──────────────┘
                        ♠ A 10 6 2
                        ♡ A 10 7 3
                        ◊ Q 10 6
                        ♣ K 2
```

You bid unopposed to Six Hearts and West leads the ◊8. How would you play?

This time, you have a two-way finesse for the queen of trumps. Should you finesse into the West hand or the East hand?

Many players would say to themselves, "West would never lead a trump if he holds the queen, but he might do so from two or three low cards." They would therefore win the diamond lead, cash the ♡A, and take a second-round finesse through West.

When the trump finesse loses, East returns a third round of trumps. Try as he might thereafter, declarer can never come to more than eleven tricks.

Rather than bank your contract on the 50-50 chance of a finesse winning, would you not prefer a line of play that will succeed more than two-thirds of the time?

The odds of a 3-2 break are 68%. If trumps split, the location of the queen is irrelevant: count your tricks – you have seven high-card winners in the side suits, so you need five trump tricks. You can afford to lose to the ♡Q: what you cannot afford is for two low trumps (which you need for ruffing) to go on the same trick.

Win the opening diamond lead and cash the ace-king of hearts. If the ♡Q falls, you can draw the outstanding trump if you wish, but it makes no difference whether you do or not. If the ♡Q has not come down, leave it outstanding and start cashing winners. Having taken all of your side-suit winners you can then crossruff the black suits for the last four tricks. A defender will be able to overruff one of these tricks with his trump winner, but that is the only trick the defense will make.

Now try your hand at another deal with a possible two-way finesse in trumps. Cover the E/W cards and decide how you would play before reading on:

N/S Vul: Dealer East

```
                    ♠ K 5
                    ♡ J 10 2
                    ◇ K J 10 2
                    ♣ Q J 7 5
♠ Q 6 3                              ♠ 7 4
♡ 9 8 7 6 3        N                 ♡ A K Q 4
◇ 8 3          W       E             ◇ 9 7 4
♣ 9 6 2            S                 ♣ A K 10 8
                    ♠ A J 10 9 8 2
                    ♡ 5
                    ◇ A Q 6 5
                    ♣ 4 3
```

West	North	East	South
—	—	1NT	2♠
Pass	2NT	Pass	3♠
Pass	4♠	All Pass	

East opens the bidding with a strong One Notrump (15-17 HCP). You overcall Two Spades and soon thereafter find yourself in game. West leads the ♡9 to East's queen and you ruff when he continues with the ♡A. How would you continue?

I would be willing to wager that most players would win the diamond and immediately play two rounds of trumps, first dummy's king and then taking the finesse on the way back: one down when West shows up with the ♠Q.

Can you see how to improve your chances?

The play to the first trick marks East with nine points in hearts. To make up the 15-17 points shown by his opening bid, he will need either the ♣A and the ♠Q or both top clubs. What he cannot have is all three missing honor cards, which would give him 18 points.

Finding out who has the high clubs is very likely to tell you the location of the queen of trumps.

Play a club to dummy's jack at trick two. East wins with the ace and continues with the king of hearts. You ruff and now play your second club. West plays low and dummy's queen forces East to reveal possession of the ♣K. He returns tries to cash the ten of clubs but you ruff and West follows suit.

You can now be fairly sure who holds the ♠Q: lead the ♠J and run it when West plays low. A spade to the king, a diamond back to hand, and the ace of spades enables you to claim a contract that would have failed had you simply followed the 'normal-looking' line of play. (Note that if West had been able to overruff with the queen on the third round of clubs, you would not have lost anything, since the alternative line play with also have failed.)

The optimum way to play a suit often depends on how many tricks you need from it, or how many losers you can afford. Cover the E/W cards and decide how you would play the trumps in this slam contract:

♠ J 7 4 3
♡ A Q
◇ Q 6 5
♣ K Q 9 5

♠ 10 9 8 5		♠ K Q 6 2
♡ J 8 7 5 4	N	♡ K 10 9 2
◇ J	W E	◇ K 9 7
♣ 10 6 2	S	♣ 7 3

♠ A
♡ 6 3
◇ A 10 8 4 3 2
♣ A J 8 4

West leads the ♠10 against Six Diamonds. Your slam is likely to depend on how you play the trump suit, so what is the best way to tackle this combination?

The answer is that you do not yet know: the optimal play in trumps depends on whether or not you can afford to lose a trump trick. You first need to find out if you have a heart to lose, so win the ♠A and lead a heart to the queen. As you can see, on the layout above the heart finesse loses. Once that happens, you are left needing to bring home the trump suit without loss. This can only be done if West holds the singleton jack of diamonds (and East the K-9-7).

You ruff East's spade return, cross to the ♡A, and call for dummy's queen of trumps. Today is your lucky day — East covers with the king and the jack falls from West. You can re-enter dummy in clubs and take the marked finesse against East's nine of trumps.

If the heart queen had won at trick two, you would then have taken the best percentage play to avoid two trump losers by cashing the ace and leading towards the queen. This would bring home the slam any time trumps were no worse than 3-1 unless East held K-J-x.

This type of "discovery play" occurs in many guises. Our next deal is a more complex variation of this same theme. Cover the E/W cards and decide how you would play:

♠ A 10 7 4 3
♡ K 8
◇ 8 6 2
♣ Q 8 5

♠ K 6		♠ Q
♡ J 10 7 5 4		♡ 9 2
◇ A 10 7 3		◇ Q J 9 4
♣ K 2		♣ 10 9 7 6 4 3

♠ J 9 8 5 2
♡ A Q 6 3
◇ K 5
♣ A J

You bid to Four Spades and West leads the ♡J — over to you.

You have five possible losers – two spades, two diamonds and one club. The optimal way to play this trump suit is to lead towards dummy, inserting the 10 if West plays the missing low spade. This ensures only one loser as long as West follows on the first round.

Let's see what might happen if you decide to set about trumps immediately: you win the heart lead in hand with the queen and play a trump. West follows with the ♠6 so you play dummy's ten. East wins with the ♠Q and switches to the ◊Q. You play the king but the ace is wrong. West wins with the ◊A, returns a diamond to his partner's jack, and East now switches to a club. You have little choice but to finesse and when West shows up with the ♣K you are one down.

Sure, it was unlucky to find both minor-suit finesses failing but this line of play fails to utilize all of declarer' resources available to declarer. A better approach is to try to combine chances. You will not be able to avoid the club finesse on this deal, so you should take it immediately: win the ♡K at trick one and play a club to your jack. West takes the ♣K and returns a second heart. Now you need to access *** 'assess' *** the relative risks – you can play either for the ◊A to be onside (50%) or for spades to divide 2-1 (significantly higher than 50%).

Win West's heart return in hand and cash the ♣A. Your objective now is to reach dummy without letting East in to play a diamond through your king. One possibility is to try ruffing your low heart, but that is not without risk. A better option is to simply play a spade to the ace. As long as both defenders follow suit you are home – you will be able to cash the ♣Q discarding one of your diamonds. It will not matter if a defender can ruff this as it will be with their natural trump trick. You will lose just one spade, one diamond and one club – ten tricks, contract made.

Quiz Hands

1.

♠ K 8
♡ A 6
◇ 8 6 4 3
♣ A 9 6 5 3

♠ A Q J 6
♡ 9 8 3
◇ A K J 10
♣ K 6

You bid unopposed to Six Diamonds and West leads the ♡K.
How should you play?

2.

♠ J 8 4
♡ 8 6 5 2
◇ A Q 5 3
♣ A 9

♠ A Q 10 9 7 6 3
♡ A 3
◇ K 7
♣ K 8

You reach Six Spades after a brisk auction and West leads the ♡Q.
How should you play?

3

♠ 9 8 4 3 2
♡ 5
◇ A 10 3
♣ A J 6 3

♠ A 7
♡ A K Q J
◇ K 9 7 6 5 2
♣ Q

You bid to Six Diamonds uncontested and West leads the ♡8.
How should you play?

4.   E/W Vul: Dealer West
                    ♠ K J 10 3 2
                    ♡ A 9 5
                    ◇ Q J 9 3
                    ♣ 8

                    ♠ A 9 7 5
                    ♡ 10 4
                    ◇ A 10 6 5
                    ♣ Q J 5

West	North	East	South
1NT	2◇*	Pass	4♠
All Pass			

1NT = 15-17; 2◇= spades and a minor

West opens with a strong (15-17) One Notrump and North rather adventurously intervenes with a bid showing spades and a minor. You take your partner's overcall a little more seriously than he intended and jump all the way to Four Spades.

West leads the ♡K.

It is now up to you to justify partner's intervention by bringing home your game.

How do you play?

Answers to Quiz Hands

1.

	♠ K 8	
	♡ A 6	
	◇ 8 6 4 3	
	♣ A 9 6 5 3	

♠ 9 7 5 4 3		♠ 10 2
♡ K Q 10 4	N	♡ J 7 5 2
◇ Q 5	W E	◇ 9 7 2
♣ 4 2	S	♣ Q J 10 8

	♠ A Q J 6	
	♡ 9 8 3	
	◇ A K J 10	
	♣ K 6	

West leads the ♡K against Six Diamonds.

Taking the diamond suit in isolation, the normal way to play would be to cash one top honor and then to finesse against the queen on the second round.

Had West been kind enough to lead a black suit, that is how you should play. Either the finesse works and you score an overtrick, or it fails and you still make twelve tricks and your contract.

On the heart lead, though, the defense has established a side-suit winner. If you now take a losing trump finesse they will be able to cash a heart to put your contract one down. Do you want to put all of your eggs into the 50-50 basket or can you see a line of play that offers better odds?

One option is to dispose of dummy's heart loser whilst keeping the trump finesse in reserve. Let's see what happens: you win the ♡A, cross to the ◇A, and then cash the king, ace and queen of spades throwing dummy's second heart. Unfortunately, East ruffs and returns the ♣Q. You now lead a second round of trumps from dummy and East produces the last outstanding low diamond.

Do you finesse against East or try to drop the ◇Q offside? Suffice it to say that you have now left yourself with a nasty guess. You may or may not do the right thing, but we seem to be back to something close to the original 50-50 decision that we were trying to avoid.

It is important that you have a basic understanding of percentages. You do not need to remember that the odds of five missing cards breaking 3-2 is 68%, but you do need to know that the chances are better than a finesse. Similarly, with three missing cards splitting 2-1 or seven missing cards being divided 4-3. Conversely, the odds of an even number of missing cards splitting evenly (ie. of four cards splitting 2-2 or six cards breaking 3-3) are worse than a finesse.

On this deal, you can avoid relying on an even money finesse and instead take the roughly 2-to-1 chance that the trumps will break 3-2. Let's see what happens if you win the ♡A and immediately cash the ace and king of diamonds. On this layout, West's queen comes tumbling down and you can draw a third round of trumps. If clubs break 3-3, you will make thirteen tricks, but you are assured of twelve and your contract.

Suppose, instead, that when you cash the two top diamonds both defenders follow twice but the queen does not appear. You can then start cashing your spade winners, throwing dummy's heart loser on the third round. Provided the defender with the ◊Q holds at least two spades, you are home. Having cashed all four spade winners, you can then cash the top clubs. You will then crossruff hearts and clubs for the last four tricks. A defender will be able to ruff or overruff with his ◊Q on one of these tricks, but that will be the only defensive trick.

2.

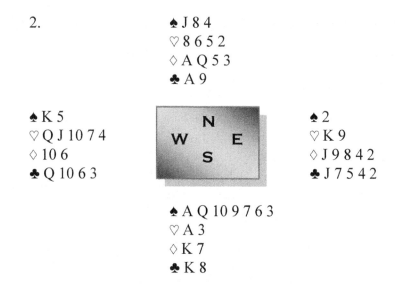

♠ J 8 4
♡ 8 6 5 2
◇ A Q 5 3
♣ A 9

♠ K 5
♡ Q J 10 7 4
◇ 10 6
♣ Q 10 6 3

♠ 2
♡ K 9
◇ J 9 8 4 2
♣ J 7 5 4 2

♠ A Q 10 9 7 6 3
♡ A 3
◇ K 7
♣ K 8

West leads the ♡Q against your spade slam.

On a minor-suit lead, you might take a trump finesse or not and you will make twelve or thirteen tricks depending on the trump position.

West's heart lead, though, exposes you to a potential second loser if the trump king is offside. You know that the odds of a 4-3 diamond break are better than the 50-50 you get from the trump finesse, so you correctly decide that you should try to dispose of your heart loser on dummy's third diamond before you risk losing the lead.

Suppose, then, that you win the opening lead with the ♡A and immediately cash your three diamond winners, taking a heart discard. Unfortunately, West is able to ruff this trick with the ♠5. That's bad news, but not necessarily fatal to your contract. You ruff the second round of hearts, cross to the ♣A, and now take the trump finesse. When West produces the ♠K, though, you are one down.

At the end of the hand, you wonder whether you should have guessed to drop West's ♠K, which was in fact singleton by the time you took the losing finesse. You might have done, but the odds are close.

There are no guaranteed lines of play here, but by far the best approach is to cash the ♠A at trick two. For a start, you might get lucky and drop the singleton ♠K offside (which is not as unlikely as you might think). You can then draw the last trump and claim. If the ♠K has not fallen but both defenders follow, you just need the player with the

♠K not to have started with a singleton diamond. All in all, fairly good odds, wouldn't you say?

3.

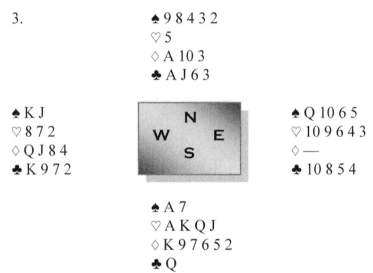

                    ♠ 9 8 4 3 2
                    ♡ 5
                    ◇ A 10 3
                    ♣ A J 6 3

♠ K J   ♠ Q 10 6 5
♡ 8 7 2   N   ♡ 10 9 6 4 3
◇ Q J 8 4   W   E   ◇ —
♣ K 9 7 2   S   ♣ 10 8 5 4

                    ♠ A 7
                    ♡ A K Q J
                    ◇ K 9 7 6 5 2
                    ♣ Q

West leads the ♡8 against your diamond slam.

You appear to have a spade to lose, which means you will need to play the trumps for no loser. Many players would get this far in their analysis and immediately set about trumps by leading to dummy's ace. When East discards on this trick, the contract is instantly doomed.

A better line is to discover if the spade loser can be avoided. At trick two, lead the ♣Q. If West covers with the king, you can win with the ♣A and pitch your spade on dummy's ♣J. If West does not cover the queen of clubs, you plan on running it – if it loses, you have only traded your unavoidable spade loser for a club loser, so nothing has been lost (and you will now need to avoid losing a trump trick) .

After West has covered the ♣Q at trick two, taking care of your spade loser your priority now is to avoid losing two trump tricks. What this means is that you can afford a safety play to guard against a 4-0 trump break. Lead a low trump from dummy, intending to play the nine from your hand if East follows with one of the missing low diamonds.

When East discards on the first round of trumps, you simply win with the king and lead a second round towards dummy's A-10, restricting East to just a single trump trick.

E/W Game: Dealer West

      ♠ K J 10 3 2
      ♡ A 9 5
      ◇ Q J 9 3
      ♣ 8

♠ 8 4		♠ Q 6
♡ K Q J 8	**N**	♡ 7 6 3 2
◇ K 8 4	**W E**	◇ 7 2
♣ A K 7 2	**S**	♣ 10 9 6 4 3

      ♠ A 9 7 5
      ♡ 10 4
      ◇ A 10 6 5
      ♣ Q J 5

West	**North**	**East**	**South**
1NT	2◇*	Pass	4♠
All Pass			

West opens a strong (15-17) one notrump but that does not stop your side bidding game. When the ♡K is led against Four Spades, can you make use of the information provided by West's opening bid to bring home your contract?

The bidding marks West with the majority of the missing points, so most declarers would simply win the opening lead, cross to the ace of spades and then finesse West for the queen. Having lost a trump trick, declarer cannot subsequently avoid losing a trick in East's side suit — one down.

A better approach is to attempt to count the high card points in West's hand. Win with the ace of hearts and immediately play dummy's club to your jack. West wins with the ♣A and continues with the queen and jack of hearts, forcing you to ruff. Who has the king of clubs? In an attempt to find out, it cannot cost to lead the queen of clubs from your hand now. Few West's will be capable of playing low in perfect tempo if they hold the king, and this West is no exception – he covers almost immediately.

It is now time to do some counting: West has shown up with six points in hearts and seven in clubs. He cannot therefore hold both the queen of spades and the king of diamonds as he is limited to 15-17 HCP.

You can now safely play a spade to dummy's king and a second round of trumps back towards your hand. As it happens, East's ♠Q appears on the second round. If the queen of spades had been with West, though, then the diamond finesse would be guaranteed to work later. By not drawing trumps immediately, you were able to get a count of the high cards before making the critical decision.

Chapter 9 – Playing Fragile Trump Suits

Playing when you have a large trump fit is relatively easy. Managing when you hold only seven or eight trumps often needs more care. The next deal appears straightforward but an experienced international player misplayed it when the hand occurred at the table, so it is worth a look. Cover the E/W hands and see if you would have done better:

None Vul: Dealer West

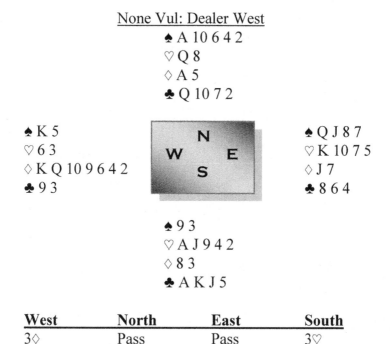

```
                    ♠ A 10 6 4 2
                    ♡ Q 8
                    ◇ A 5
                    ♣ Q 10 7 2

  ♠ K 5                              ♠ Q J 8 7
  ♡ 6 3               N             ♡ K 10 7 5
  ◇ K Q 10 9 6 4 2  W   E          ◇ J 7
  ♣ 9 3                S            ♣ 8 6 4

                    ♠ 9 3
                    ♡ A J 9 4 2
                    ◇ 8 3
                    ♣ A K J 5
```

West	North	East	South
3◇	Pass	Pass	3♡
Pass	4♡	All Pass	

West opens Three Diamonds and you essay Three Hearts in the pass-out seat. Partner raises to game and West leads the ◇K. You win in dummy and advance the ♡Q, covered by king and ace. Now what?

Declarer now tried the ♡J and a third trump, hoping either that the ten would fall or the suit would divide evenly. It was not to be and East scored both his ♡10 and ♡7. The defense still had winners in spades and diamonds to come: one down.

Appreciating the value of intermediate cards is always important, and particularly so in a less-than-robust trump suit. Cashing the jack on the second round of trumps had the effect of wasting the power of dummy's ♡8. Had declarer simply played a low trump from hand at trick three, the defense would have been powerless to take more than one trump trick and the contract would have succeeded.

It is not unusual to find yourself with a rather feeble trump suit in low level contracts. An uncontested auction such as 1♠-1NT-2♠ will often leave you in the sort of contract we see on the next deal:

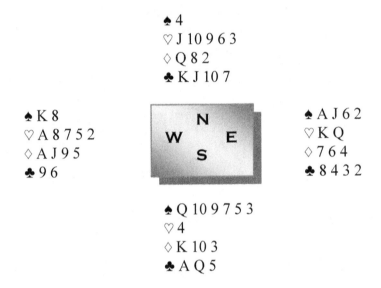

      ♠ 4
      ♡ J 10 9 6 3
      ◇ Q 8 2
      ♣ K J 10 7

♠ K 8   ♠ A J 6 2
♡ A 8 7 5 2   **N**   ♡ K Q
◇ A J 9 5 **W** **E** ◇ 7 6 4
♣ 9 6   **S**   ♣ 8 4 3 2

      ♠ Q 10 9 7 5 3
      ♡ 4
      ◇ K 10 3
      ♣ A Q 5

West leads the ♣9 against Two Spades. How should you play?

The opening lead suggests you should set about trumps immediately as a defensive club ruff is likely to leave you with little chance. To maximize your chances in the trump suit, win the opening lead in dummy (with the ♣10) and lead a trump, inserting the ♠10 when East plays low. West wins with the ♠K (marking East with the jack) and continues with a second club. This trick you should win in hand with the ace in order to play a second round of trumps.

Which spade should you lead on the second round? Any spade will work if the suit splits 3-3. What about if one of the defenders began with a doubleton, though?

The best card is the ♠Q, which will limit your losses to three trump tricks if either the jack (with East) or the eight (with West) is now singleton. East wins with the ♠A as West follows with the eight. East now cashes the ♡K and continues with the ♡Q. You ruff and lead the ♠9, driving out East's jack as West discards a heart.

East returns a club and West shows out: it is safe to cash dummy's fourth club winner, so you overtake the ♣Q and cash the ♣J, throwing a diamond. When you now play a diamond to the king, West wins and returns a diamond to dummy's queen. You score the remaining two tricks with your 7-5 of trumps over East's lone six.

Bidding in today's game is much more competitive than it was in yesteryear. You rarely get a free ride and everyone is reluctant to let you play at a comfortable level. If you are going to bid aggressively, though, your play has then to justify your optimism. N/S reached game on the next deal. Would you have managed to bring the contract home? Cover the E/W cards if you want to test your skill as declarer:

None Vul: Dealer South

```
              ♠ 9
              ♡ Q 10 8 7 4
              ◇ J 9 8 6 3
              ♣ Q 5

♠ K 6                          ♠ A Q 10 8 5 2
♡ J 9 6 5        N             ♡ A
◇ Q 10 4      W     E          ◇ A 7 5
♣ 10 9 8 4       S             ♣ 6 3 2

              ♠ J 7 4 3
              ♡ K 3 2
              ◇ K 2
              ♣ A K J 7
```

West	North	East	South
—	—	—	1NT
Pass	2◇*	2♠	3♡
Pass	4♡	All Pass	

147

After a strong One Notrump opening and a transfer to hearts, East enters with a spade overcall. You show your fit with a Three Heart bid and your partner takes a shot at game. West leads the ♠K and switches to the ♣10 at trick two. How would you play?

Faced with developing a two-suited hand, it is usually right to set about establishing the side suit early. With that in mind, you win the club switch in dummy with the queen and take advantage of the entry to lead a diamond towards your hand. Luck is on your side: East goes in with the ace and returns a diamond to the king. Now what?

It is now time to think about playing trumps, but first you should do some counting. West might well have competed over your Three Hearts with ♠K-x-x (or he may have led low from three) so East is likely to hold six spades. He has also shown up with two diamonds and is fairly likely to hold a third (West played the ten on the second round and probably would not have done so from Q-10-x-x). What is happening in clubs? East followed with the ♣2 on the first round and he may have played high-low with a doubleton.

On balance, it seems that East rates to hold only one or two hearts. As he is also favorite to hold the ace, you would prefer to lead the first trump through him. Cross to dummy with a spade ruff and lead a heart towards your king.

East wins this trick with the ♡A and plays the ♠A on which West throws a club as you ruff in dummy.

You can now ruff a diamond with the remaining low trump in your hand and lead winning clubs. Whether West ruffs the fourth round or not does not matter – if he does so, you can overruff and then ruff dummy's last diamond with the ♡K. You lose only to the three missing aces: contract made.

Note that you only ever played one round of trumps on this deal, and that was after you thought you knew roughly how the suit would lie. You essentially nullified West's potentially killing trump holding by leading winners through him in the endgame.

Landing in a less than robust trump fit is not unusual when the opponents make you guess by cramping the auction. On our next deal, you find yourself in game with only seven trumps. Cover the E/W cards and decide how you would play:

N/S Game: Dealer West

```
                    ♠ K 7 4
                    ♡ A 9 5 3
                    ◊ 8
                    ♣ A Q 10 7 3

 ♠ 9 5                  N              ♠ 10 8 6 2
 ♡ J 8 6 2      W              E       ♡ Q 10
 ◊ K Q J 9 4           S              ◊ A 7 6 2
 ♣ 8 6                                 ♣ K 4 2

                    ♠ A Q J 3
                    ♡ K 7 4
                    ◊ 10 5 3
                    ♣ J 9 5
```

West	North	East	South
2◊	Dble	4◊	4♠
All Pass			

At favorable vulnerability, West opens with a weak two bid in diamonds that is described as 5-9 HCP and a five or six card suit. Your partner doubles and East ups the ante to the 4-level. Deciding that the available penalty rates to be inadequate compensation for a vulnerable game, you take a shot at Four Spades.

West leads the king of diamonds and continues with the queen. Having ruffed in dummy, how would you play?

Looking at just the N/S hands on their own, you might conclude that you need either the spades to break 3-3 or the club finesse to work. Drawing trumps (four rounds if necessary) and then taking the club finesse is certainly one possible line of play.

Even breaks in side suits are less likely than normal when the opponents have pre-empted, so you would be particularly lucky to find the trumps splitting here. As to the club finesse, the odds are surely that it will fail now that West has already shown up with a significant portion of his high-card allocation in the diamond suit.

If trumps split 4-2 and the ♣K is offside, this line of play will see

149

you going two or three down (depending on whether the opponents' diamonds divide 5-4 or 6-3). Can you see a more promising alternative?

There are numerous possibilities, but only one that guarantees the contract provided trumps divide no worse that 4-2. The answer is quite straightforward once you realize that you are willing to lose one club trick and one trump: see what happens if you ruff the diamond at trick two and then simply play the ace and another club.

Either defender may be able to win with the ♣K and play a third round of the suit for their partner to ruff. The clubs are now established, though, and dummy still has a low trump to protect you from a third round of diamonds. You will be able to win the return, draw trumps, and eventually cross back to dummy with the ♡A to discard any red-suit losers you have left on dummy's long clubs.

Sometimes, your trump suit might not be as strong as you would like even when you have the auction to yourself:

Both Vul: Dealer South

♠ A 7 5 4
♡ K 10 6 2
◇ 8 5
♣ Q 10 5

♠ K J 9		♠ Q 10
♡ 8 5 3		♡ Q J 9 4
◇ Q J 10 9		◇ 6 4 2
♣ A 9 7		♣ 8 6 4 2

♠ 9 6 3 2
♡ A 7
◇ A K 7 3
♣ K J 3

West	North	East	South
—	—	—	1NT
Pass	2♣	Pass	2♠
Pass	4♠	All Pass	

West leads the ◇Q against your Four Spade. How would you play?

Suppose you win the opening diamond lead and immediately play ace and another spade. West overtakes his partner's queen of spades with the king on the second round of trumps and then cashes a third round with the jack before playing a second diamond. You can set up your club winners by knocking out the ace now, but when the defense play a third round of diamonds you have to ruff with dummy's last trump. In addition to two trumps and the ace of clubs, you are also going to have a diamond loser left at the end: one down.

Trying, instead, to ruff two diamonds before drawing trumps does not work either: East will score an overruff and West will still have two natural trump tricks. It seems that drawing trumps leads to failure but so too does not drawing them. What alternative is there?

What you really want to do here is to play two rounds of trumps without the defenders being able to play a third round. First, though, you need to establish your side-suit winners, so win the opening diamond lead and immediately play a club. (If the defenders do not take their ace of clubs, you must play a second round of the suit, risking the ruff.)

You win the diamond continuation and now set about trumps, but you are not going to play the ace on the first round. Let the defenders win the first spade by playing low from dummy.

Whatever the defense does now, you are in control. Suppose they switch to hearts: win in hand with the ace of hearts and play a second round of trumps to dummy's ace. You can now cash your remaining heart and club winners and then crossruff your red-suit losers. The defenders will be able to ruff or overruff one of these tricks with their remaining high trump, but that will be only their third and last trick: ten tricks, contract made.

Quiz Hands

1.

E/W Game: Dealer South

♠ J 7 5 2
♡ 9
♢ Q 7 4
♣ A J 7 5 4

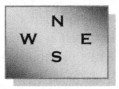

♠ A
♡ Q 8 6 4 3 2
♢ A K 8
♣ 8 6 3

West	North	East	South
—	—	—	1♡
Pass	1♠	Pass	2♡
All Pass			

West leads the ♢10.
How do you play?

2.

♠ K 7 4
♡ A K 5
◇ A 10 4
♣ J 6 5 4

♠ 8 6 5 3 2
♡ 8 7
◇ J
♣ A K Q 10 3

You reach Four Spades in an uncontested auction.
West leads the ♡Q.
How would you play?

Answers to Quiz Hands

1.

E/W Game: Dealer South

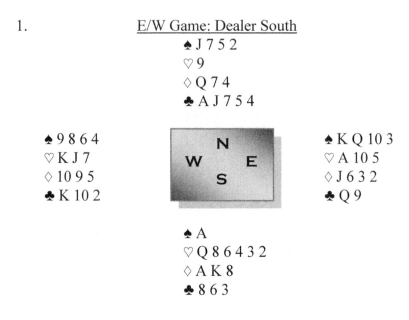

```
                  ♠ J 7 5 2
                  ♡ 9
                  ◊ Q 7 4
                  ♣ A J 7 5 4

♠ 9 8 6 4                             ♠ K Q 10 3
♡ K J 7          N                    ♡ A 10 5
◊ 10 9 5      W     E                 ◊ J 6 3 2
♣ K 10 2         S                    ♣ Q 9

                  ♠ A
                  ♡ Q 8 6 4 3 2
                  ◊ A K 8
                  ♣ 8 6 3
```

West	North	East	South
—	—	—	1♡
Pass	1♠	Pass	2♡
All Pass			

West leads the ◊10 against your lowly Two Heart contract.

When you hold a long, ragged trump suit there are two options: try to draw trumps or leave trumps alone and instead attempt to score tricks by ruffing.

Even when your suit is extremely weak, leading trumps whenever possible is usually the best approach. Remember that in a 6-1 fit, after the first round of trumps you can fell two of the defenders trumps for only one of yours.

Win the opening diamond lead with the queen and lead dummy's singleton heart. If the defenders win and persist with their diamond attack, win in hand and lead a second round of trumps. If the defense plays a spade or a diamond next, you will win and play a third heart. If they switch to clubs, win with dummy's ace and get back to your hand with the ace of spades to lead trumps again. You will eventually make three heart tricks to go with three diamonds and the two black aces: eight tricks and contract made.

2.

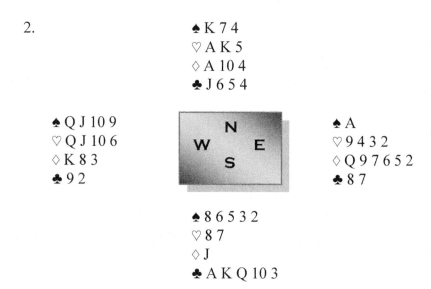

♠ K 7 4
♡ A K 5
◇ A 10 4
♣ J 6 5 4

♠ Q J 10 9
♡ Q J 10 6
◇ K 8 3
♣ 9 2

♠ A
♡ 9 4 3 2
◇ Q 9 7 6 5 2
♣ 8 7

♠ 8 6 5 3 2
♡ 8 7
◇ J
♣ A K Q 10 3

West leads the ♡Q against your Four Spade contract.

The biggest danger here is that some of your clubs winners will get ruffed, so you clearly need to set about drawing some trumps even though your spades are weak. How should you attempt this?

You have no losers in the side suits, so how many trumps can you afford to lose?

You are in the relatively unusual position of being able to lose three trump tricks. What you cannot afford is to lose four!

You can get to your hand either by leading a club or by taking a ruff in one of the red suits. Shortening your trumps does not seem like a particularly good idea. However, crossing in clubs risks giving the defense a chance to take a ruff with a non-trump trick.

More to the point, though, is that you do not want to play the king on the first round of trumps. What if the suit is distributed as in the diagram above? By playing the ♠K on the first round, you take an unnecessary risk. Will the finesse not work just as well on the second round of trumps if West holds the ace?

Let's see how the play should go: win the opening heart lead and play a low spade from dummy. If the cards are as shown, East's ace falls on fresh air and your king will restrict West to just two trump tricks later. Nothing is lost if, instead, East's singleton trump is a lower one. You will win the heart continuation, cross to your hand in clubs, and lead the second round of spades towards dummy. Whether West plays his ace now or let's dummy's king win this trick makes no difference. If the defenders are able to take a club ruff at this stage then the trumps will have broken 3-2 and that ruff will be only their third and last trump winner.

Chapter 10 – Overcoming Bad Breaks

How often do you hear: "I couldn't make it because the trumps didn't break"? It is a common refrain and yet you have probably noticed that expert players often seem able to overcome such misfortune.

To illustrate the point, take a look at this deal played by French multiple World Champion Catherine D'Ovidio at the 2008 Mind Sports Olympiad in Beijing:

N/S Game: Dealer South

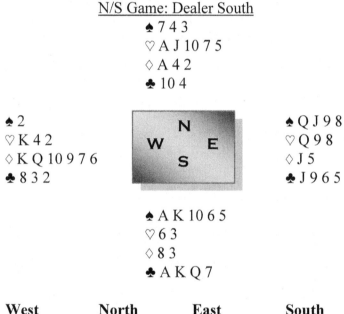

♠ 7 4 3
♡ A J 10 7 5
♢ A 4 2
♣ 10 4

♠ 2
♡ K 4 2
♢ K Q 10 9 7 6
♣ 8 3 2

♠ Q J 9 8
♡ Q 9 8
♢ J 5
♣ J 9 6 5

♠ A K 10 6 5
♡ 6 3
♢ 8 3
♣ A K Q 7

West	North	East	South
—	—	—	1♠
3♢	3♠	Pass	4♠
All Pass			

West leads the ♢K. How would you play?

Declarer won the opening lead in dummy with the ♢A and led a trump to the ace. After cashing two high clubs, she then ruffed her low club in dummy, both defenders following suit. When declarer then played dummy's last trump, East put in the jack and declarer won with the ♠K as West discarded a diamond.

It looks as if declarer must lose two trump tricks in addition to one trick in each red suit. Can you see how the French maestra made ten tricks from here?

With six tricks already in the bag (two high trumps, the ◊A, two high clubs and a club ruff in dummy) and the ♡A and ♣Q to come, declarer needed to score two of her remaining three trumps.

D'Ovidio cashed the ♣Q, East having to follow suit, and then played her remaining diamond. West won and switched to a heart, but declarer won with dummy's ♡A and led a third round of diamonds. East could not profitably ruff so he discarded a heart, which allowed declarer to score a low trump. She then exited with her second heart and waited to score a trick at the end with her ♠10. Chapeau!

On our next deal, a bad trump break seems to leave declarer with two unavoidable losers. See if you can see how to make one of them disappear as if by sheer magic:

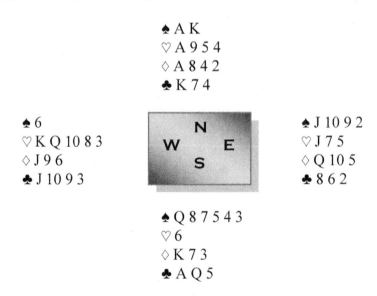

```
                    ♠ A K
                    ♡ A 9 5 4
                    ◊ A 8 4 2
                    ♣ K 7 4

  ♠ 6                                   ♠ J 10 9 2
  ♡ K Q 10 8 3          N               ♡ J 7 5
  ◊ J 9 6          W         E          ◊ Q 10 5
  ♣ J 10 9 3            S               ♣ 8 6 2

                    ♠ Q 8 7 5 4 3
                    ♡ 6
                    ◊ K 7 3
                    ♣ A Q 5
```

If spades split 3-2, there are twelve easy tricks in both spades and notrumps. There are advantages to playing the suit slam, though. How would you play Six Spades on the lead of the ♡K?

158

You win the opening lead with the ace of hearts and cash dummy's top spades. When West discards on the second round of trumps, you seem to have two unavoidable losers, one trump and one diamond.

Can you see any way home?

The experienced player would realize that all is not lost so long as East holds at least three clubs. Your first task is to reduce your trump length to the same as East, so ruff a heart, play three rounds of clubs ending in dummy and ruff another heart. When you then cash the king and ace of diamonds these cards remain:

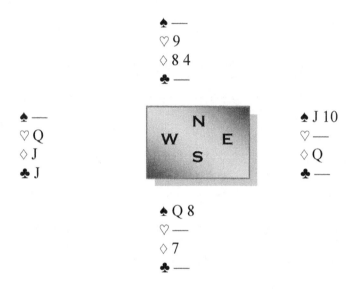

Leading the heart from dummy leaves East with no recourse. If he ruffs, you will discard your losing diamond and make the last two tricks with the Q-8 of trumps. If, instead, East discards his diamond, you will ruff with the ♠8 and the queen of spades will be your twelfth trick.

So what happened to those two losers? Effectively, the defenders' spade and diamond winners both fell on the same trick. Magic!

Sometimes, declarer's trump suit will appear even more robust. On what type of deal, do you suppose, is it most important for declarer to make a conscious effort to stop and think before playing?

Of course, ideally declarer should always make a thorough plan before even calling for a card from dummy at trick one, but there is one particular situation when even experienced players sometimes fail to do so — the type of deal to which I refer is one on which the contract looks easy. To see what I mean, decide how you would tackle this next deal as declarer?

N/S Vul: Dealer South

♠ 5
♡ 6 3
♢ K 9 5 3
♣ 10 7 6 5 3 2

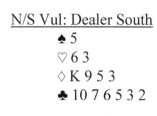

♠ K 7
♡ A K Q J 10
♢ A 10 8 4 2
♣ A

West	North	East	South
—	—	—	1♡
2♠	Pass	3♠	4♢
4♠	5♢	All Pass	

You reach Five Diamonds in a competitive auction and West leads the ♠Q to his partner's ace. The ♣Q is returned. How would you play?

Perhaps your first thought is to wonder how you might have bid a slam. After all, you only need trumps to split 2-2 and you will have twelve tricks. However, I hope that this is not the only thinking that you do before banging down a top trump.

Rather than wasting mental energy thinking about the auction, about which you can now do nothing, you should instead be concentrating on how to make at least eleven tricks in Five Diamonds. If it occurs to you to stop and ask yourself, 'what can go wrong?' you should conclude that the principal danger is a 4-0 trump split.

If you immediately cash the ◊A and West shows out, you will then be unable to avoid losing two trump tricks to East. Perhaps, then, you should instead start by leading a low trump from hand at trick three.

West follows with a low diamond and it then occurs to you that although he will hold six or seven of the ten missing spades, it is not impossible that West also began with all four missing trumps.

Then you get a 'Eureka' moment and the light goes on – if you just cover West's low trump with dummy's ◊9, you will ensure a maximum of one trump loser irrespective of how the suit splits.

Let us stop to look at this diamond suit in isolation. The textbook safety play to ensure that you avoid two losers in this suit is to start by leading low from either your hand or dummy. Assuming that the next opponent follows with a low card, you simply cover his card. By playing the diamond suit in this manner, you can restrict your losers in the suit to a maximum of one no matter how the suit divides.

The problem, of course, is that you rarely have the luxury of playing a suit in isolation. You always need to play it in the context of the whole deal.

Declarer on the next deal had learned the safety play in this suit but he missed an important point. You have doubtless heard the expression, 'a little learning is a dangerous thing' and declarer learned how true this can be at the bridge table. This was the full deal:

♠ 5
♡ 6 3
◊ K 9 5 3
♣ 10 7 6 5 3 2

♠ Q J 10 9 6 3 2   ♠ A 8 4
♡ 8 5   ♡ 9 7 4 2
◊ J 7 6   ◊ Q
♣ 8   ♣ K Q J 9 4

♠ K 7
♡ A K Q J 10
◊ A 10 8 4 2
♣ A

East won trick one with the ♠A and switched to the ♣Q. Declarer won with the ♣A and led a low diamond from hand. When West followed with the six, declarer thought he could safely guard against a 4-0 trump split by playing dummy's nine. East won the trick with the ◇Q and played the ♣4. Declarer ruffed but East overruffed with the ◇J to set the contract.

If this rather unfortunate turn of events had happened to you, ask yourself what lesson you would learn from the experience. For many players, having just failed in a contract that the rawest beginner would bring home, the conclusion they might reach is that the old guy who taught them about safety plays obviously didn't know what he was talking about. It is, however, quite correct to make a safety play on this deal. Let's go back and see what thought process declarer missed.

East's play of the ♣Q, concealing the king, was thoughtful, but declarer should not have been lulled into a false sense of security. It is not sufficient to ask 'what can go wrong in diamonds?' Rather, declarer must always think of the entire deal, and a 5-1 club break is certainly not an impossibility. Does, this mean that the safety play in diamonds is wrong? No, but you need to lead the first round of trumps from dummy in case clubs break badly.

Having won trick two with the ♣A, declarer should cross to dummy by ruffing his ♠K! He then leads a low trump, intending to cover with the ◇10 if East follows with a low trump. By taking the precaution of starting trumps from dummy, declarer ensures that only West can gain the lead on the first round of trumps. West is the safe hand – no return that he can make after winning the first round of trumps can hurt you.

As it happens, East will play the queen on the first round of trumps, so you can win with the ace and take a second-round guess for an overtrick. Your contract, though, is safe.

Yes, I know that those of you who banged down the ◇A or led a diamond to the king at trick three also made eleven or twelve tricks. You should, however, just count yourself lucky to have done so. Next time, a defender may show out on the first round of trumps. And, if this happens to you often enough, you may start remembering to ask 'what can go wrong?'

Now cover the E/W cards and try your hand at a grand slam:

```
              ♠ A K J 9
              ♡ A Q 7 4
              ◇ K 6
              ♣ K 6 2

♠ —                              ♠ 8 6 5 3 2
♡ J 9 8            N             ♡ 10 6 3 2
◇ J 10 8 5 3   W     E           ◇ 9 7
♣ Q 10 8 4 3      S              ♣ J 9

              ♠ Q 10 7 4
              ♡ K 5
              ◇ A Q 4 2
              ♣ A 7 5
```

You bid well to reach the excellent contract of Seven Spades. With only twelve top tricks, a small slam is likely to be the limit in notrumps, but it looks like a red-suit ruff will deliver your thirteenth trick playing in a spade contract.

West leads the ◇J to dummy's king and you immediately lay down the ace of spades. If trumps break 3-2 you will be able to claim fairly quickly. West follows with a black card on the first round of trumps and it takes a moment for your brain to register that he has played a club rather than a spade. Disaster! Now you will never be able to draw all of East's trumps. How would you continue?

The first thing to do at this stage is to make sure that you follow the excellent advice offered regularly by Sergeant Jones from the classic British sitcom *Dad's Army*: "Don't Panic!"

Now that you are back in 'thinking mode', can anything be done to overcome this foul trump break?

The good news is that East's trumps are all relatively small. The contract can still be made as long as East has no singletons and at least three cards in one of the red suits. Can you see how?

The first thing you must do is to cash two high-card winners in each side suit (to prevent East making a killing discard). You also need to complete this process ending in the dummy.

Having played one round of trumps and the ace-king of all three side suits, you can now lead the ♡Q from dummy. If East ruffs this, you plan to overruff and try to cash the ◊Q, throwing dummy's remaining club. When East has to follow to the third rounds of hearts, you discard the club loser from your hand.

You can now lead dummy's last heart and ruff in your hand. East follows suit, leaving him with only trumps. When you ruff a diamond in dummy, East has to underuff, and you can then lead dummy's club and overruff East's card. You have two high trumps left for the final two tricks: contract made despite the 5-0 trump split.

Sometimes the auction forewarns you of a bad break. Take a look at the next deal and see if you can take advantage of the information you have been given:

None Vul: Dealer South

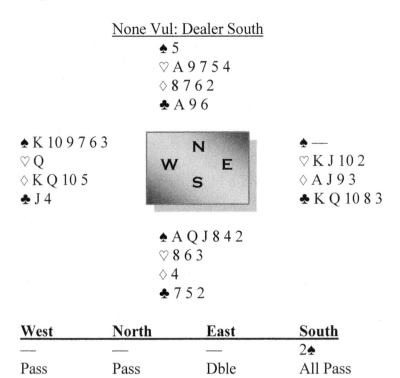

```
                    ♠ 5
                    ♡ A 9 7 5 4
                    ◊ 8 7 6 2
                    ♣ A 9 6

♠ K 10 9 7 6 3          N              ♠ —
♡ Q                                     ♡ K J 10 2
◊ K Q 10 5      W            E          ◊ A J 9 3
♣ J 4                   S               ♣ K Q 10 8 3

                    ♠ A Q J 8 4 2
                    ♡ 8 6 3
                    ◊ 4
                    ♣ 7 5 2
```

West	North	East	South
—	—	—	2♠
Pass	Pass	Dble	All Pass

You open with a weak two bid in spades and East's takeout double ends a brief but eventful auction. West leads two rounds of diamonds against Two Spades Doubled. How would you play?

West's pass of his partner's takeout double is easily understandable, and it is not hard for you to guess that the trumps are not lying favorably for you. Or are they?

Actually, it can be to declarer's advantage when a defender has a trump holding such as the one East has here, as he will frequently become what is known as 'trump bound'. Your first objective is to score however many low trumps you can by ruffing. So, ruff the second round of diamonds, cross to dummy with one of the aces and ruff another diamond, then repeat the process with dummy's other ace. You have now scored five tricks and still hold A-Q-J of spades. Now is the time to try to force West to take the lead by exiting with any one of your plain-suit losers.

East can win this trick as West plays his last non-trump but the end is nigh. Having no trump to play, East must play a heart or a club next and West is forced to ruff his partner's winner and lead a trump around to your jack. When you then exit with another loser, West will again have to ruff and lead into your tenace.

You have made all six of your trumps plus dummy's two aces: eight tricks and contract made despite West's huge trumps stack.

You might notice that West could have beaten this contract by switching to a heart or a club at trick two, restricting you to two diamond ruffs. In contracts such as this (where the trumps break very badly), declarer usually wants to score his small trumps by ruffing. As a defender, be aware of this and do not help declarer's cause by forcing him to ruff.

Quiz Hands

1.

None Vul: Dealer West

♠ A Q
♥ A 8 7 4
♦ A K 4 3
♣ A K 3

♠ K 9 7 6 4
♥ 3
♦ 7 6 5
♣ 9 8 6 2

West	North	East	South
1♥	Dble	Pass	1♠
Pass	2♥	Pass	2♠
Pass	3NT	Pass	4♣
Pass	4♠	Dble	All Pass

West opens the bidding and after you wend your way to Four Spades on a 7-card trump fit East expresses his doubts about the contract's viability.

West leads the ♥ K against Four Spades-Doubled.

How should you play?

166

2.

♠ A J 5 3
♡ A 9
◇ K 6
♣ A Q J 9 2

♠ K 9 7 2
♡ 4
◇ A Q 7 4 3
♣ K 10 6

West	North	East	South
—	—	2♡	Dble
4♡	5♡	Pass	5♠
Pass	6♠	All Pass	

East/West hike the auction up to the 4-level in front of North's good hand, leaving your side to guess at an uncomfortable level.

North goes for the jugular with his raise to slam and West leads the ♡J against Six Spades.

How should you play to justify your partner's aggressive view?

Answers to Quiz Hands

1.

None Vul: Dealer West

♠ A Q
♡ A 8 7 4
◇ A K 4 3
♣ A K 3

♠ 5
♡ K Q J 10 9 6
◇ Q J 9 2
♣ Q 5

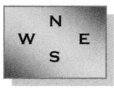

♠ J 10 8 3 2
♡ 5 2
◇ 10 8
♣ J 10 7 4

♠ K 9 7 6 4
♡ 3
◇ 7 6 5
♣ 9 8 6 2

West leads the ♡K against Four Spades Doubled.

You judged correctly that 3NT would fail, but Four Spades is no picnic either and East's double suggests that you will not be favored with an even trump split. Partner seems to have been mesmerized by all those high-card points: can you justify his optimistic bidding?

You have five side-suit winners and three top trumps. To make ten tricks, you will therefore need to score both of your low trumps.

Win the heart lead with dummy's ace and immediately ruff a heart. The bidding warns you that East may now have run out of hearts, so it is time to cash dummy's minor-suit winners before he can take a damaging discard. When you then lead a third heart from dummy, what can poor East do?

Unless he ruffs high, you will score a second low trump right now. He does the best that he can by ruffing with the ♠10 but you overruff with the king, cross back to dummy with a trump, and play a fourth round of hearts. Whatever East does, he cannot stop you scoring a trick with the nine of spades.

East has three black winners left, and West has three winners in the red suits. Alas for the defense, their goodies all crash together.

The type of play is known as an 'elopement'. You score your low trumps and leave one defender ruffing his partner's winners at the end.

2.

                    ♠ A J 5 3
                    ♡ A 9
                    ◇ K 6
                    ♣ A Q J 9 2

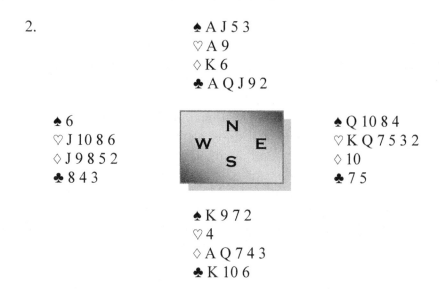

♠ 6   ♠ Q 10 8 4
♡ J 10 8 6   ♡ K Q 7 5 3 2
◇ J 9 8 5 2   ◇ 10
♣ 8 4 3   ♣ 7 5

                    ♠ K 9 7 2
                    ♡ 4
                    ◇ A Q 7 4 3
                    ♣ K 10 6

West leads the ♡J against Six Spades.

Unlike the previous deal, this time you seem to have plenty of tricks so you need to ask yourself "What could go wrong"?

You should come to the conclusion that you contract will be safe as long as you avoid losing two trump tricks.

You might decide that you should win the ace of hearts, lead a spade to the king, and then finesse the jack on the second round. You can even handle a 4-1 spade break assuming that it will be East, who opened with a weak two in hearts, who may be short in spades.

That is a not unreasonable assumption, but it is also an unnecessary one here. In fact, you are able to guard against either defender holding four spades with this trump combination.

To ensure playing this spade suit for a maximum of one loser (assuming no 5-0 break) you should start by cashing the high honor accompanying the jack (i.e. the ace here). You can then lead a second round of trumps towards the remaining K-9-x holding in your hand. If East follows suit, you intend to play the nine. Whether it wins or loses, you will be assured of only one loser in the suit.

As the cards lie, East inserts the ten on the second round of spades. You win with the king but West discards. It is vital that you now continue with the ♠9 from your hand to force out East's queen. Note that if you now lead your low spade to dummy's jack, East can win with the ♠Q and return a heart, forcing you to ruff with your nine, thus promoting his eight into the master trump.

By playing the nine, you retain the master trump (the jack) in dummy. If East then returns a heart, you can ruff with your last low trump, enter dummy in a minor suit, and draw his remaining trump. If he does anything else, you will draw his trump and discard dummy's heart loser on the third round of diamonds.

Note that if East had discarded on the second round of trumps, you would still be okay: you would win with the king and lead a third round towards dummy's remaining J-x, restricting West to just one trick with his queen-ten combination.

Chapter 11 – The Ace of Trumps

Forget the nominal value assigned to the various honors by the point-count system. Although you will have counted it as only four high-card points, the ace of your trump suit is a special case and is often worth much more than it's *a priori* value. As we shall see, timing when to use this vital resource can be just as important when you are defending as when you become declarer.

Take a look at these two possible trump suits...

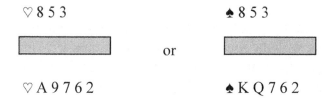

$\heartsuit$ 8 5 3 $\spadesuit$ 8 5 3

or

$\heartsuit$ A 9 7 6 2 $\spadesuit$ K Q 7 6 2

You will have counted only four HCPs for the hearts on the left but five for the spades on the right. Which, though, would you rather have as your trump suit?

In the heart suit above, you clearly have two inescapable trump losers, even assuming that the suit splits evenly.

Playing in the spade suit, you might escape for just one trump loser, given a 3-2 break, a favorable position of the ace, and sufficient entries to dummy.

That's obviously a plus for the spades, so let's take a look at a couple of deals involving trump suits like these:

```
                      ♠ K 7 3
                      ♡ 8 5 3
                      ◇ A 4 2
                      ♣ Q 8 5 4

  ♠ J 10 2              ┌─────────┐            ♠ Q 9 8 6 4
  ♡ K J 4              │    N    │            ♡ Q 10
  ◇ J 9 7 6            │  W   E  │            ◇ 10 5
  ♣ A 9 2              │    S    │            ♣ J 10 7 3
                       └─────────┘

                      ♠ A 5
                      ♡ A 9 7 6 2
                      ◇ K Q 8 3
                      ♣ K 6
```

West leads the ♠J against your Four Heart contract. How would you play?

You must assume that trumps will break 3-2 (otherwise your contract has no chance). Counting your losers, you can see two in trumps and the ace of clubs on top. You will also need to do something with the fourth diamond in your hand.

At first glance it seems that you will need diamonds to break 3-3, which rates to happen only slightly more than one time in three. Can you see how you might improve on those odds?

How about ruffing the fourth round of diamonds in dummy?

You will need to time the play correctly: win the spade lead in hand with the ace and immediately duck a round of trumps by leading a low heart from your hand. East wins with the ♡10 and plays a second spade to dummy's king. You now lead a second round of trumps to your ace, both defenders following suit.

You are now just about home and it is time to set about diamonds. Cash your three winners in the suit and, when the suit fails to divide, lead the losing fourth diamond from your hand to ruff in dummy. The defenders will to make their trump winner at some point: it matters not whether they ruff one of your high diamonds, overruff dummy on the fourth round, or save their trump winner for later.

Having taken care of that losing diamond, you can then play a club to establish your winner in that suit. West can take this trick and cash his winning trump, but the rest are yours – ten tricks irrespective of how the diamonds split.

If you look at just this heart suit on its own, it may not seem to matter when you play the ace. This deal illustrates, though, that this is not the case – play the ace too early and you lose control and go down, time its use correctly and you bring home your contract.

By changing the deal slightly we can see how controlling the trump suit is equally vital whether you are declaring or defending:

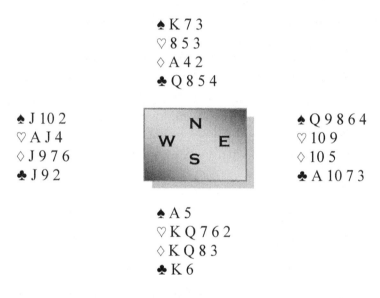

```
                ♠ K 7 3
                ♡ 8 5 3
                ◊ A 4 2
                ♣ Q 8 5 4

♠ J 10 2            N              ♠ Q 9 8 6 4
♡ A J 4        W        E         ♡ 10 9
◊ J 9 7 6          S              ◊ 10 5
♣ J 9 2                           ♣ A 10 7 3

                ♠ A 5
                ♡ K Q 7 6 2
                ◊ K Q 8 3
                ♣ K 6
```

Once again, you declare Four Hearts on a spade lead.

This time, you choose to win in dummy with the ♠K in order to lead a trump towards your hand. East follows with the ♡9 and your king wins the trick. Looking for an extra entry to dummy, perhaps you try a low club next, but dummy's queen loses to East's ace and a second spade comes back to your ace.

With only one entry to dummy remaining, you cross to the ◊A and play a second trump. East follows with the ♡10 and you try the queen, but West wins this trick with the ace. All would be well if West played a black suit now but, instead, he cashes the ♡J, removing dummy's final trump. He then exits with a club to the king and your only remaining chance is to find the diamonds breaking 3-3. When they fail to do so, you are one down.

You lost the same two trump tricks and one club as on the first variation of the deal, but this time you also had to lose a diamond. You could have tried to avoid losing a diamond by abandoning trumps after the first round and playing ◊K, ◊A and a third round of diamonds from dummy Whether East ruffs this trick with his ♡10 or waits and overruffs dummy on the fourth round of diamonds makes no difference, though – you will lose a third trump trick and finish one down.

The problem on this deal is that you could not control how many trumps were played. You wanted to play exactly two rounds of trumps before switching to diamonds. Note that had West made the mistake of taking his ♡A on the first round of the suit, you would then have been in the same position as declarer on the first layout. By withholding his ace, though, West gave declarer a choice between playing one round of trumps or three, both of which were losing options.

Let's take a look at another example. Cover the E/W cards and decide how you would play before reading on.

♠ Q 6
♡ A J 9 4
◊ A J 9 3
♣ A 6 2

<table>
<tr>
<td>
♠ J 8 5 2
♡ Q 10 3
◊ 7
♣ J 9 8 7 4
</td>
<td>
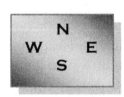
</td>
<td>
♠ A 9 7 4
♡ K 5
◊ 10 8 6 5 2
♣ 10 5
</td>
</tr>
</table>

♠ K 10 3
♡ 8 7 6 2
◊ K Q 4
♣ K Q 3

Three Notrumps would be an ideal spot but, as often happens when you have a 4-4 fit in a major, you get to game in that suit. West leads the ◇7 against your Four Heart contract. How would you play?

Taking this heart suit in isolation, the percentage play to lose the minimum number of tricks (i.e. one) is to start with a deep finesse of the nine, playing West for either Q-10-x or K-10-x. Having forced East's high honor on the first round, you then take a second-round finesse with the jack against West's remaining honor.

Let's see what happens: you win the opening diamond lead in hand with the queen and lead the ♡2. When West follows with the ♡3 you put in dummy's nine. The good news is that East wins with the ♡K. The bad news is that when he returns a diamond, West ruffs with the ♡10, plays a spade to his partner's ace, and is dealt a second ruff with the ♡Q. You have lost one spade and three trumps: one down.

How could you have done better?

The important thing to realize on this deal is that you do not need to play the trumps for only one loser: you can afford to lose two trump tricks in addition to the ♠A and still make your contract. What you cannot afford is three trump losers, so it is imperative that you play two rounds of trumps as quickly as possible.

You should win the diamond lead in hand and immediately lead a trump to the ace. You could simply lead a second trump from dummy now, but you would then be relying solely on a 3-2 break. With adequate entries to your hand, you can still take precautions against West having started with K-Q-10-4 of trumps by crossing back to your hand with a high club in order to lead the second round of trumps towards dummy's jack. When both defenders follow to the second round of trumps, your contract is assured. (Curiously, had dummy's trumps instead been ♡A-5-4-3, the correct play would be more obvious — possession of the jack-nine combination provided a losing alternative.)

As we saw earlier, it is frequently right to duck the first round of the suit when you hold the ace of trumps as a defender. Declarer may not be able to risk a second round of trumps for fear that you will then play a third round. Even if you hold only a doubleton ace, remember that declarer does not know this. (When your ace is doubleton, you may still be able to get to your partner's hand anyway in order to play a third round of trumps.)

Of course, there are exceptions to every general rule. The obvious case is when the defenders can take ruffs with their low trumps. This variation on the deal above illustrates:

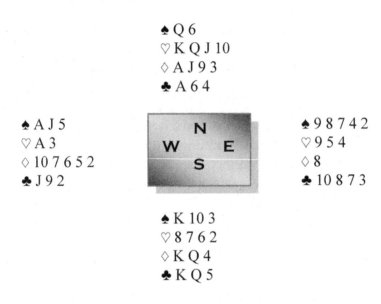

♠ Q 6
♡ K Q J 10
♢ A J 9 3
♣ A 6 4

♠ A J 5
♡ A 3
♢ 10 7 6 5 2
♣ J 9 2

♠ 9 8 7 4 2
♡ 9 5 4
♢ 8
♣ 10 8 7 3

♠ K 10 3
♡ 8 7 6 2
♢ K Q 4
♣ K Q 5

This time, dummy's trumps are much more robust, but you are missing the crucial ace.

West again leads the ♢7 against Four Hearts. You win in hand and play a trump but West steps up with his ace and leads a second diamond for East to ruff. A spade to West's ace allows him to deliver a second ruff to defeat the contract. The same defense will work whichever defender holds a singleton diamond and three trumps as long as his partner holds both missing aces.

On the first version of this deal, declarer could avoid losing three trump tricks by playing two rounds of the suit immediately. In the second, he did not have that option because he was missing the ace of trumps.

There is only one version of the next deal, but once again it illustrates the importance of the ace of trumps. If you're up for a challenge, cover the E/W cards and see if you can spot the winning line of play:

Both Vul: Dealer West

```
              ♠ A 9 7
              ♡ 3
              ◇ 9 8 7 4
              ♣ Q 9 5 4 2

♠ —                              ♠ K 5 2
♡ K Q 10 9 8 4        N          ♡ J 5
◇ J 6 5 2        W         E      ◇ Q 10 3
♣ 8 7 3               S          ♣ A K J 10 6

              ♠ Q J 10 8 6 4 3
              ♡ A 7 6 2
              ◇ A K
              ♣ —
```

West	North	East	South
2♡	Pass	Pass	4♠
Pass	5♡	Pass	6♠
All Pass			

West leads the ♡K against your slam. How would you play?

You seem to have four possible losers – the ♠K and three hearts. Playing on trumps does not rate to be a winning line of play, so you decide you need to ruff all three of your heart losers.

Let's see what happens: you win the opening lead with the ♡A and ruff a heart with dummy's ♠7. Returning to your hand with a club ruff, perhaps you now ruff your penultimate heart with dummy's ♠9. Unfortunately, East is able to overruff this trick with the ♠K and he rudely returns a trump. No matter what you do from here on, you will be left with a losing heart at the end: one down.

What could you have done differently?

You were always happy to lose a trick to the ♠K, but in order to take care of all three of your heart losers you needed to ruff three times with dummy's trumps, including once with the ace. Note the difference if, instead of ruffing the third round of hearts with dummy's nine, you ruff with the ♠A. You can then return to your hand with a second club ruff and ruff your last heart with the ♠9. Whether East overruffs at this point or saves his ♠K for later matters not a jot. The king of trumps will be the defenders' only trick: twelve tricks made.

West's opening bid here warned you that East was likely to hold at most two hearts, but it was a warning that should not be needed. You plan to ruff heart with all three of dummy's trumps anyway, so there is no reason to save the ace for the third ruff. Even without any opposition bidding, this would be the correct way to play the hand.

Quiz Hands

1.
    ♠ A 7 6
    ♡ J 10 6 4 2
    ◇ A 9 4 3
    ♣ 8

    ♠ 8
    ♡ A Q 7 5 3
    ◇ K 6
    ♣ A 7 5 3 2

West leads the ♠Q against Six Hearts.
How should you play?

2.
    ♠ A 5
    ♡ A
    ◇ A K Q J 6 3
    ♣ K 8 5 3

    ♠ Q J 10 8 6 4
    ♡ 8 6 3
    ◇ 4
    ♣ A 6 2

You open the bidding with a weak two and soon find yourself in slam. West leads the ♡K against Six Spades. How should you play?

Answers to Quiz Hands

1.

```
                    ♠ A 7 6
                    ♡ J 10 6 4 2
                    ◊ A 9 4 3
                    ♣ 8

♠ Q J 10 4 2          N          ♠ K 9 5 3
♡ K 9          W            E     ♡ 8
◊ Q 10 7 5          S          ◊ J 8 2
♣ J 6                           ♣ K Q 10 9 4

                    ♠ 8
                    ♡ A Q 7 5 3
                    ◊ K 6
                    ♣ A 7 5 3 2
```

West leads the ♠Q against Six Hearts.

Having won the opening lead with dummy's ace of spades, you lead the ♡J and East follows with the eight. Do you finesse?

There are layouts where finessing will be right (e.g. K-x-x of hearts and a singleton diamond with East and clubs 4-3), but they are a rarity. More likely is something like the distribution diagrammed above.

You have four top tricks outside the trump suit, so you should look for a way to make eight trump tricks. Playing the ace on the first round of trumps can win in two ways. Firstly, you might drop a singleton king in the West hand. More likely, West will follow with a low trump leaving one of the defenders with the lone ♡K. You now have eight trumps remaining between your hand and dummy and you need seven of them to win.

That seems like an ideal scenario – you can ruff all four of your losing clubs in dummy using spade and diamond ruffs as re-entries to your hand. One of your trumps will get overruffed by the ♡K, leaving you with eight trump tricks (the ace plus the seven ruffs that win) to go with your four outside winners: slam made.

If you had taken a trump finesse at trick two, West would win and return a trump, telescoping two of your remaining eight trumps into a

180

single trick. When clubs failed to split you would then have been a trick short and your slam would have failed.

2.

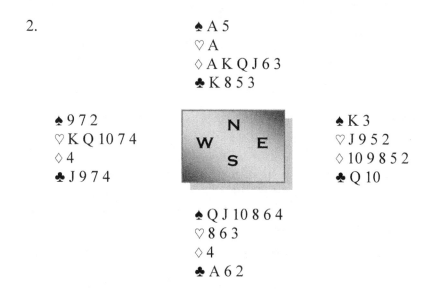

```
                        ♠ A 5
                        ♡ A
                        ◇ A K Q J 6 3
                        ♣ K 8 5 3

    ♠ 9 7 2                                  ♠ K 3
    ♡ K Q 10 7 4            N               ♡ J 9 5 2
    ◇ 4              W             E         ◇ 10 9 8 5 2
    ♣ J 9 7 4               S               ♣ Q 10

                        ♠ Q J 10 8 6 4
                        ♡ 8 6 3
                        ◇ 4
                        ♣ A 6 2
```

West leads the ♡K against Six Spades.

On a minor-suit lead, declarer would have had an easy ride – win in dummy and play ace and another spade to drive out the king. The ♣A then provides an entry to draw the remaining trumps, and declarer's rounded-suit losers will subsequently go on dummy's diamond winners.

The heart lead presents a stiffer challenge. How can declarer draw trumps without allowing the defense to cash heart tricks? Some declarers might attempt to discard their losers before drawing trumps but, with West holding a singleton diamond, this is not a successful option.

Did you think about crossing to the ♣A in order to take a spade finesse? Unfortunately, when the finesse loses, East returns a club to remove dummy's last outside entry to the diamonds. Declarer can cash the ♠A and then try to cash diamonds, but West ruffs the second round and cashes a couple of heart and/or club tricks to defeat the contract.

To bring home your slam, you need to use the ace of trumps to keep control of the hand in unusual fashion. Notice what happens if you win the ace of hearts and immediately lead the low trump from dummy.

Holding only a doubleton king of spades, East is forced to take his trump trick immediately or lose it. Whether he then forces dummy to ruff or switches makes no difference as long as you are careful. The most testing defense is a club return: you must win in hand with the ace, unblock the ♠A, cash one high diamond, then ruff the second round of diamonds high. Having drawn the last trump you can then reenter dummy with the ♣K to discard your losers on the remaining high diamonds.

Suppose a defender had held three spades to the king and had ducked the first round. You would still have been okay as long as the defender with the ♠K held at least two diamonds – win the ♠Q, cross to the ♠A and start cashing diamonds throwing hearts.

This deal illustrates not only the power of the ace of trumps but also the importance of thinking creatively as declarer. It was a particularly difficult deal, though, so don't worry too much if you didn't spot the solution — you won't be alone.

Chapter 12 – Plays Involving Entries

Entry management is often a crucial factor when planning the play. Decisions about whether to draw trumps immediately will often be influenced by entry considerations. In previous chapters we have established the importance of drawing trumps in order to avoid getting your winners ruffed, but there are exceptions to every rule. Take a look at this deal:

E/W Vul: Dealer South

```
                    ♠ A 6 2
                    ♡ K 5 3
                    ◇ 7 6 4 3
                    ♣ 8 5 4
♠ Q J 10 4                              ♠ K 9 8
♡ 8 4 2            N                    ♡ 9 7
◇ K 2         W         E               ◇ Q 8 5
♣ J 9 7 6          S                    ♣ K Q 10 3 2
                    ♠ 7 5 3
                    ♡ A Q J 10 6
                    ◇ A J 10 9
                    ♣ A
```

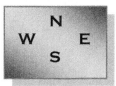

West	North	East	South
—	—	---	1♡
Pass	2♡	Pass	4♡
All Pass			

West leads the ♠Q against Four Hearts. How do you play?

You have two unavoidable spade losers, so the fate of your contract seems to depend on playing the diamond suit for one loser. That goal will be achievable as long as East to holds one of the diamond honors won't it?

Note what happens, though, if you immediately draw trumps after winning the first or second round of spades. You can finish drawing trumps in dummy in order to play a diamond. How, though, do you plan to take a second finesse in the suit?

In view of the limited entries to dummy, you must play the first round of diamonds immediately. Assume West wins and the defense take their spade tricks and exit with a club. You can now draw trumps, ending in dummy, and repeat the diamond finesse.

Now you are warmed up, try your hand at another heart game:

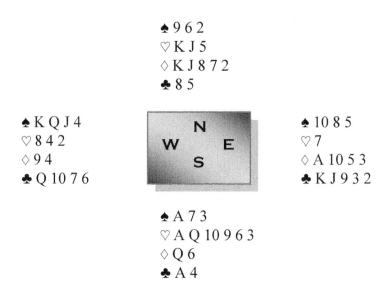

```
                ♠ 9 6 2
                ♡ K J 5
                ◇ K J 8 7 2
                ♣ 8 5

♠ K Q J 4          N              ♠ 10 8 5
♡ 8 4 2        W       E          ♡ 7
◇ 9 4              S              ◇ A 10 5 3
♣ Q 10 7 6                        ♣ K J 9 3 2

                ♠ A 7 3
                ♡ A Q 10 9 6 3
                ◇ Q 6
                ♣ A 4
```

West leads the ♠K against Four Hearts.

How do you play?

The opening lead exposes two fast spade losers, but a quick count suggests that you still have enough tricks. So you win the ♠A and start drawing trumps by cashing the ace and playing a second round to dummy's king.

When East discards a club on the second round of trumps, you do not have to be Mystic Meg to foresee what will happen if you now draw West's last trump — when you then play diamonds, East will take his ace on the second round of the suit and switch to clubs. You will have a winning diamond in dummy but no way to reach it. In the fullness of time, the defense will make a club trick and your contract will fail.

Since the only potential entry to dummy's third-round diamond winner is in trumps, you need to establish that winner before using your vital entry. After taking two rounds of trumps you must switch tacks and set about driving out the ◊A. East can hold off his ace until the second round of diamonds and the defenders can cash their two spade winners but you are then in control. Even if East plays a third round of diamonds you can ruff with a high trump from your hand.

Having regained the lead you can then cross to dummy, drawing West's last trump in the process. Your club loser will now disappear on dummy's remaining diamond winner: ten tricks and contract made.

Judging whether to win a particular trick may determine the success of your contract. So, too, can the choice of where to win. Because it is your longest and strongest suit, your trump suit will often be needed for transportation purposes. Look at this suit layout:

♠ K J 9 7

♠ A Q 10 8 2

Suppose that you are playing in a spade contract: West cashes a high diamond and continues the suit for you to ruff in your hand. Do you automatically ruff with your smallest trump?

Before deciding which trump to use for your ruff, you first need to analyze the entry situation on the deal as a whole. Suppose, first, that this is the full layout:

♠ K J 9 7
♡ A Q J 6
◇ 9 7
♣ A Q J

♠ 5
♡ K 7 5 2
◇ K Q 5 2
♣ K 10 7 6

♠ 6 4 3
♡ 10 8
◇ A J 10 8 6 3
♣ 9 2

♠ A Q 10 8 2
♡ 9 4 3
◇ 4
♣ 8 5 4 3

With dummy holding tenace positions in both rounded suits, you are going to need plenty of entries to your hand if you are to make the maximum number of tricks. With spades your only high cards, you will need to maximize trump entries to your hand.

Ruffing the diamond at trick two with the small trump provides you with a potential five possible trump entries. Every time you get the lead in your hand you need to make use of that entry, by taking a finesse.

As you hold an equal number of cards in each of the two side suits, it doesn't matter which you attack first, so let's suppose you take a heart finesse. When that wins, you can re-enter your hand by drawing the first round of trumps. Be careful, though, not to waste any of the valuable spots in your hand – whichever trump you lead from dummy, just cover it: you can lead the ♠K and overtake it with the ace or play the ♠7 to your eight.

The important thing is to keep as many trump entries to your hand as possible.

Back in your hand for a second time, you can now take a club finesse. That also wins, so you now draw a second round of trumps, again preserving your entries. You can now repeat the heart finesse and, when it wins again, you can now draw the final trump whilst simultaneously reaching your hand for a fourth time.

After repeating the winning club finesse you can claim: twelve tricks made irrespective of how the side suits split.

The next layout looks similar, but this time the tenaces are in your hand and it is dummy that needs entries:

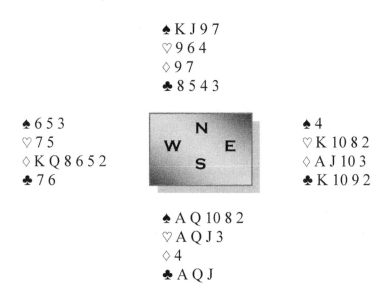

♠ K J 9 7
♡ 9 6 4
◇ 9 7
♣ 8 5 4 3

♠ 6 5 3
♡ 7 5
◇ K Q 8 6 5 2
♣ 7 6

♠ 4
♡ K 10 8 2
◇ A J 10 3
♣ K 10 9 2

♠ A Q 10 8 2
♡ A Q J 3
◇ 4
♣ A Q J

Once again, West leads two rounds of diamonds against your spade contract. With which trump are you going to ruff this time?

Looking at the relatively bereft dummy, it should be clear that you desperately need trump entries there. By ruffing with the ♠A at trick two, you can ensure four natural trump entries to the dummy.

As before, you can lead any trump from your hand as long as you overtake as cheaply in dummy: so lead the ♠2 and win with dummy's seven or lead the ♠Q and overtake with the king, for example.

In dummy for the first time, take a heart finesse. When that wins, cross back to dummy again cheaply in trumps and take a club finesse.

Now draw the defenders' last trump whilst returning dummy for the third time. It does matter which finesse you take next: repeating the winning heart finesse allows you to cash the ♡A and then ruff the fourth heart (whether it is a winner or not) in order to return to dummy for a fourth time to repeat the club finesse; twelve tricks again. (Note that if you repeat the club finesse when you use your third trump entry to dummy, you will have no way to re-take the heart finesse, since you will have no route back to dummy.)

Now that you have the idea of using the trump suit to move back and forth between your hand and the dummy, cover the E/W cards and see if you can find your way to ten tricks on this deal:

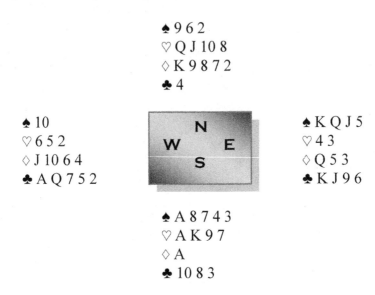

♠ 9 6 2
♡ Q J 10 8
◇ K 9 8 7 2
♣ 4

♠ 10
♡ 6 5 2
◇ J 10 6 4
♣ A Q 7 5 2

♠ K Q J 5
♡ 4 3
◇ Q 5 3
♣ K J 9 6

♠ A 8 7 4 3
♡ A K 9 7
◇ A
♣ 10 8 3

You reach Four Hearts in an uncontested auction and West leads the ♠10.

How should you play?

If this deal was played at a large number of tables, I would guess that a high proportion of declarers would effectively go down at trick two: seeing the singleton in dummy, they would immediately play a club to set up ruffs in that suit. As long as the defenders win the club and return a trump, the contract can then no longer be made.

Rather than rush in, instead start by counting your tricks: you currently have only three side-suit winners and four trumps tricks, so you need to generate three additional tricks. It is easy enough to arrange to score a couple of ruffs, but that will still leave you one trick short. To bring your total of tricks up to the ten required you will also need to establish a long card in one of the side suits.

Suppose, first, that you try to score a trick with dummy's fifth diamond. The obvious first move is to cross to the ◇A, thus unblocking the suit. You can then set about drawing trumps and, since

188

you need entries to dummy, you do this by leading a low trump from your hand. Cashing the ◊K now avoids any chance of getting that card ruffed later. You can then ruff a diamond (being sure to do so with either the ace or the king). Leading your second low heart returns you to dummy and enables you to take a second diamond ruff, with your last trump.

You can now exit with a black suit, allowing the defenders to cash their three winners. Dummy will be left with two winning trumps and the thirteenth diamond. Eventually, you will ruff a black suit lead, draw the outstanding trump, and score the long diamond at trick thirteen. Game bid and made.

Entries, or the lack of them, are also the key on our next pair of deals. This time, though, the gaps are in the trump suit itself:

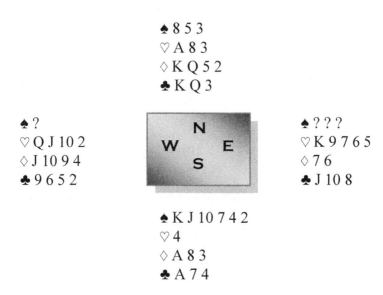

```
              ♠ 8 5 3
              ♡ A 8 3
              ◊ K Q 5 2
              ♣ K Q 3

♠ ?                            ♠ ? ? ?
♡ Q J 10 2       N             ♡ K 9 7 6 5
◊ J 10 9 4    W     E          ◊ 7 6
♣ 9 6 5 2        S             ♣ J 10 8

              ♠ K J 10 7 4 2
              ♡ 4
              ◊ A 8 3
              ♣ A 7 4
```

You reach Six Spades with no opposition bidding and West leads the ♡Q. How do you play?

The fate of your contract depends upon restricting your trump losses to just the ace. At trick two, you lead a trump from dummy and East follows low. Should you put up the king or take the finesse by inserting the jack?

With nothing else to guide you, this is a purely mathematical problem. If the defenders' spades break 2-2 with the honors divided, then the odds are exactly even whether West hold the doubleton ace or the doubleton queen. What about when West holds a singleton or void spade, though?

Playing the king is the winning play only if West holds specifically the singleton queen of spades. If he has a singleton ace, a low singleton or even a void, though, playing the king will leave you with two trump losers.

If, instead, you put in the jack, it does not matter whether West wins with the ace, follows with a low card or even discards: you will be able to return to dummy in a minor and lead a second round of trumps. Whether East began with two, three or four spades including the queen, taking the finesse will bring home the contact. The finesse is, therefore, more than a 3:1 favorite.

Now take a look at this deal with an identical trump suit:

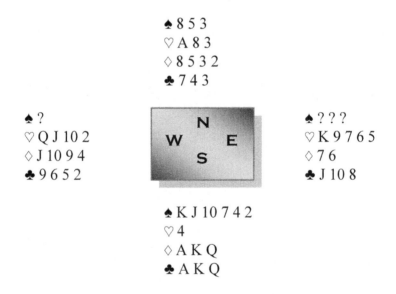

```
                 ♠ 8 5 3
                 ♡ A 8 3
                 ◇ 8 5 3 2
                 ♣ 7 4 3

♠ ?                   N                ♠ ? ? ?
♡ Q J 10 2      W           E          ♡ K 9 7 6 5
◇ J 10 9 4            S                 ◇ 7 6
♣ 9 6 5 2                              ♣ J 10 8

                 ♠ K J 10 7 4 2
                 ♡ 4
                 ◇ A K Q
                 ♣ A K Q
```

Again, you play in Six Spades on the lead of the ♡Q.

How do you now play?

As before, the fate of the contract depends solely on avoiding two trumps losers. This time, though, you are in dummy with the ♡A for the first and last time. You lead a low trump and East follows with a low card.

Should you play the king or take the finesse?

Once again, if the trumps split 2-2 then it is a straight 50-50 guess. What if trumps are not 2-2, though?

Now, there is only one layout of the defenders' cards that allows you to make the contract – a singleton queen in the West hand. If West holds a singleton ace, a low singleton or a void spade, you are destined to go down irrespective of what you do, since you cannot get back to dummy in order to pick up a guarded trump queen in the East hand.

On this layout, therefore, rising with the king gives you the best percentage chance of bringing home your slam.

Entries are also a consideration when deciding how you should play the trump suit on our next deal. Cover the E/W cards and see if you can make up for partner's exuberant bidding with some stellar declarer play:

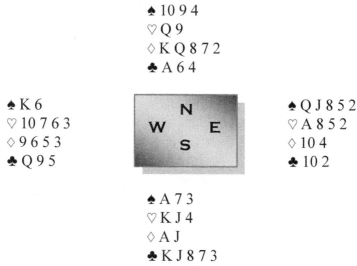

```
                    ♠ 10 9 4
                    ♡ Q 9
                    ◇ K Q 8 7 2
                    ♣ A 6 4

♠ K 6                  N              ♠ Q J 8 5 2
♡ 10 7 6 3      W           E        ♡ A 8 5 2
◇ 9 6 5 3              S              ◇ 10 4
♣ Q 9 5                              ♣ 10 2

                    ♠ A 7 3
                    ♡ K J 4
                    ◇ A J
                    ♣ K J 8 7 3
```

Perhaps you would rather have settled in 3NT, but partner was seduced into a slam hunt by his excellent controls and you instead end up in a precarious minor-suit game. West leads the ♠K against your Five Club contract.

How do you play?

The first question is what to do at trick one. You are not going to be able to avoid losing a trick the ace of hearts. If you let the defenders score a spade trick, you will then have to play the trumps for no loser.

The optimum way to play this club suit without loss is to cash the ace and finesse on the second round. Having done that, though, even if you find East with a doubleton or trebleton ♣Q, how are you going to get back to dummy to cash the diamonds? It looks like you will need also the diamonds to break 3-3, so that you can overtake the jack on the second round.

Those don't seem like great odds. Can you spot a better strategy?

Curiously, your trumps are too good: possession of the ♣J is actually a red herring on this deal as it risks leading you down the wrong path – the best line of play would be easier to spot if the trumps in your hand were just K-x-x-x-x. You can afford to allow the defenders to make a trump trick, provided that you do not also lose a spade.

Let's see what happens: win the ♠A at trick one, draw one round of trumps with the king and then unblock the diamonds by cashing both the ace and jack. Now it is time to use that vital entry to dummy, by playing a trump to the ace. Both defender follow and you are nearly home. (Notice that it does not matter if the ♣Q falls or not.) All you need now is for the defender with the outstanding trump to have started with at least three diamonds.

You cash the ◊K, and although East shows out he does not ruff. You discard a spade on this trick, and another on the ◊Q. You then switch to hearts. You will lose just the ♡A and a trump: Five Clubs bid and made. What's more, it is possible that 3NT may have failed on a spade lead.

Trumps are incredibly versatile things. This does mean, though, that you have to decide which of their attributes you need to employ on a particular deal. We all make the mistake of playing on autopilot sometimes, and many declarers would suffer a blind spot on our next deal. Your first inclination on seeing dummy will not always be right, so remember to think through the whole hand before you commit yourself.

Neither Vul: Dealer South

```
                    ♠ ---
                    ♡ Q 7 4 3
                    ◇ 8 6 4
                    ♣ A Q J 10 9 4

    ♠ A J 9 8 6          N           ♠ K 10 7 4 2
    ♡ A 8 2        W           E     ♡ 6
    ◇ Q 10 5 3           S           ◇ J 9
    ♣ 6                              ♣ 8 7 5 3 2

                    ♠ Q 5 3
                    ♡ K J 10 9 5
                    ◇ A K 7 2
                    ♣ K
```

West	North	East	South
—	—	—	1♡
1♠	3♣	4♠	6♡
All Pass			

West leads the ♣6 against your heart slam. How do you play?

Counting losers, you can see one heart, two diamonds and three spades – that seems like an awful lot when you are in a slam contract. Perhaps, therefore, your first inclination is to reduce that number by ruffing a spade or two in dummy?

Let's see what happens if you try that: after winning with the ♣K, you ruff a spade and lead a trump. Your king is allowed to win and you are in hand again, so you ruff a second spade. Now you can cross to the ◇A and ruff your last spade. Alas, when you next cash a club, discarding one of your diamond losers, West ruffs. He then draws dummy's last trump with the ♡A and you are left with a diamond loser — one down.

Let's go back to the beginning and think again: dummy has five club winners on which you can dispose of all of your spade and diamond losers. In order to enjoy those winners, though, you will need to be able to reach dummy after trumps are drawn. The problem is that

West's opening club lead has removed your club entry, which means that you only route to dummy is in trumps. That spade ruff that we were so keen to take as quickly as possible needs to wait until it is most useful – after the defenders' trumps have been drawn.

If you simply play a trump at trick two, what can West do? If he ducks, you will play a second trump. Whatever happens, you will be able to score four trumps in hand, two diamond winners and six club tricks – slam made!

On the previous deal it was a case of when to use a crucial entry. Sometimes the entry itself will not be apparent. See if you can spot how to bring home your game contract on the next deal:

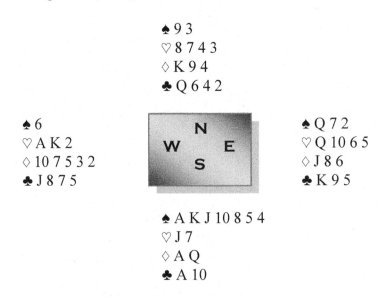

♠ 9 3
♥ 8 7 4 3
♦ K 9 4
♣ Q 6 4 2

♠ 6
♥ A K 2
♦ 10 7 5 3 2
♣ J 8 7 5

♠ Q 7 2
♥ Q 10 6 5
♦ J 8 6
♣ K 9 5

♠ A K J 10 8 5 4
♥ J 7
♦ A Q
♣ A 10

You quickly reach Four Spades against which West leads the ace, king and a third heart. How do you play?

You have four possible losers, two hearts and one in each black suit. Of course, the queen of trumps may well come down, solving your problems. What can be done, though, if she is not so obliging?

One not unreasonable line of play would be to ruff the third round of hearts and cash the top spades, but if the queen fails to appear your chances are very slim. Fortunately, though, there is a much more promising line of play available – by giving one of the defenders a choice of poisons, both of which are equally fatal for his partnership.

Suppose that after ruffing the third round of hearts you immediately unblock the diamonds by cashing the ace and queen. All you need to do now is to reach dummy in order to make use of the ◊K. One option is to take an unusual trump finesse by leading a low spade towards dummy. If West holds the ♠Q he will be unable to stop you. Can you see a line of play that is much better than this 50% shot though?

How about leading the ♠J from your hand at trick six?

What is poor East to do? If he takes his queen of trumps now, you can win the return and cross to dummy with the ♠9 in order to discard your club loser on the king of diamonds. Alternatively, he can allow the ♠J to win, but then of course you will promptly cash the ace and king of trumps, felling his queen, and the club winner at the end will be only the third trick for the defenders. Either way, you will emerge with ten tricks and your game.

Some plays are quite tricky to spot if you haven't seen them before. Try to remember the first time someone showed you how to make two tricks with A-Q opposite a doubleton – that is now filed away in your brain under 'obvious', so have a look at this variation:

> ♠ K 5 2
> ♡ J 6 2
> ◊ A K 8 3
> ♣ K 7 4

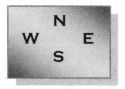

> ♠ A Q J 10 6
> ♡ A K 5
> ◊ J 4
> ♣ A 8 5

West leads the ♡10 against Six Spades.
How do you play?.

Despite plenty of high-card points and a more-than-adequate trump suit, the two hands do not fit well and there seem to be only eleven tricks. All is not lost -- the ♡Q may drop and, failing that, perhaps you can generate a twelfth trick via a squeeze of some sort. Those don't seem like particularly good odds, though.

Dummy's square shape means that there are no additional tricks to be made from ruffing, so perhaps you start by drawing trumps. You then set about cashing some winners but when the ♡Q fails to appear on the second round and no squeeze materializes you find that you are one down.

Could anything have been done?

Did you think about taking a finesse?

If you don't see a finesse, go back and look at the diagram once again. Can you see the finesse now?

When I presented this deal to my intermediate class and told them to take 'the finesse' they scratched their collective heads and eventually tried leading the ♡J from dummy. That, though, is not a finesse – to finesse you have to lead *towards* the honor you wish to promote.

The finesse in this deal is nothing quite as obvious as an A-Q combination, but take a closer look at that diamond suit. When you first look at this deal, it seems as if you are in danger of losing a trick in both hearts and clubs. Your best chance of producing twelve tricks, though, is to lose one trick in diamonds and none in any of the other suits.

Let's see what happens if you win the opening heart lead with the ace and then cash two top trumps from your hand. East discards a club on the second round of trumps, but that's okay. You continue with a third round of trumps to dummy's king and must now make use of that entry by leading a low diamond towards your jack. If East holds the ◊Q, what can he do?

Suppose he takes this trick and returns a club: you must be careful to win this in hand with the ace (preserving dummy's entry). You can now draw the last trump and cash the ◊J. The ♣K provides access to the ace-king of diamonds, on which you discard your losing club and losing heart.

Voila! Twelve tricks.

The winning play on our next hand is not obvious at first glance either. The deal originated in the "Young Chelsea Marathon", a grueling 24-hour matchpointed pairs event, and illustrates that even when your trump suit splits evenly you may still need some luck to land your contact:

♠ K Q 4
♡ 10 7 2
◊ 5
♣ Q J 9 8 5 3

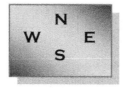

♠ A 10 8 6 2
♡ 9 4
◊ A K 2
♣ A 7 2

You play in Four Spades and West leads the ♡5 to his partner's king. East cashes the ♡A and then switches to the ♣4. How would you play?

The first question to address is 'What is the most likely club position?'

With an easy heart continuation available and a diamond switch unlikely to give much away, it seems unlikely that East has switched away from the ♣K. His switch to the lowest missing spot is much more likely to be a singleton. So, what are we going to do about that?

Your first instinct may be "go up with the ace of clubs, draw trumps, then knock out the ♣K".

Counting your tricks, though, should tell you that this strategy is destined to fail. Assuming, as we have, that West holds three clubs to the king, he will simply duck the second round of the suit. Having already drawn trumps, there will then be no entry to dummy's long clubs. We will have only nine tricks – five trumps, two diamonds and two clubs. In addition to two hearts and a club, we will also have to

197

lose a diamond at the end.

To bring the total back to ten, we need to ruff the diamond loser. Before doing so, though, can you see the problem that will arise?

Suppose you win the club switch with the ace, cash the top diamonds and ruff a diamond with the ♠4. After cashing one of dummy's remaining trumps, these cards will then remain:

♠ K
♡ 10
♢ ---
♣ Q J 9 8

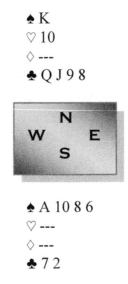

♠ A 10 8 6
♡ ---
♢ ---
♣ 7 2

Can you see the problem?

When you cash the ♠K, the lead will still be in dummy and you cannot get back to your hand to draw the last trump without allowing the opponents in. If East (who started with a singleton club) has the missing trump, he will now be able to get a club ruff. So, what are the alternatives?

Well, nothing is certain, but success at bridge is all about playing the percentages. With West holding the singleton club he is more likely to hold the spade length and, therefore, the ♠J. Take a look at the full hand opposite: can you now see how you can make the contract if, as expected, East holds the singleton club and three trumps to the jack?

```
              ♠ K Q 4
              ♡ 10 7 2
              ◇ 5
              ♣ Q J 9 8 5 3

♠ 9 3                              ♠ J 7 5
♡ Q 8 6 5        N                ♡ A K J 3
◇ Q 10 9 6   W       E            ◇ J 8 7 4 3
♣ K 10 6         S               ♣ 4

              ♠ A 10 8 6 2
              ♡ 9 4
              ◇ A K 2
              ♣ A 7 2
```

You need to win the ♣A at trick three and then play three rounds of diamonds, ruffing the third round in dummy with a high trump. You can cash dummy's remaining high trump and then finesse the ♠10 on the second round of the suit. If East follows to this trick with the last low trump, you will be conveniently in your hand. You can now draw the missing trump before you have to let the defenders in when setting up your second club trick.

Of course, the trump finesse may fail, but if you lose to a doubleton jack of spades in the West hand, then so be it. The suggested line of play wins (with the alternative failing) whenever East holds three trumps including the jack. The reverse is true when it is West who holds three trumps to the jack. With the clubs 3-1, though, it is more likely that East holds three trumps and it is therefore a better percentage shot to ruff high and take the trump finesse.

Quiz Hands

1.
   ♠ A 9 4
   ♡ A 6
   ◇ 8 5 4
   ♣ 8 7 5 3 2

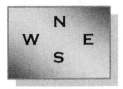

♠ K Q J 6 2
♡ J 3
◇ A K 7
♣ A 9 4

West leads the ♣K against Four Spades. You win the ♣A and return a club at trick two. West wins as East discards a heart, and West now switches to the ♡K. How do you continue?

2.
   ♠ 10 8 5
   ♡ 10 7 4 3
   ◇ J 6
   ♣ A K 3 2

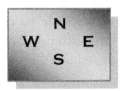

♠ A J 9 6 2
♡ Q 8 5 2
◇ A K Q
♣ Q

West leads the ♣J against Four Spades. How do you play?

3.

♠ 8
♡ J 6
◇ A 7 5 4
♣ A K Q 9 5 3

♠ A K Q J 9 6
♡ 8 5 3
◇ J 9 2
♣ 4

West leads three top hearts against Four Spades.
How do you play?

4.

♠ A K 5 3 2
♡ 8 6 4 3
◇ 5
♣ 7 5 2

♠ Q 9 7 6
♡ A K
◇ A Q 7
♣ A Q 6 4

You declare Six Spades after West has opened the bidding with a
weak two in hearts.

West leads the ♡Q. What is your plan?

1.

$\spadesuit$ A 9 4
$\heartsuit$ A 6
$\diamondsuit$ 8 5 4
$\clubsuit$ 8 7 5 3 2

$\spadesuit$ 10 7 3 $\spadesuit$ 8 5
$\heartsuit$ K Q 9 $\heartsuit$ J 10 8 7 5 2
$\diamondsuit$ J 10 3 $\diamondsuit$ Q 9 6 2
$\clubsuit$ K Q J 10 $\clubsuit$ 6

```
        N
    W       E
        S
```

$\spadesuit$ K Q J 6 2
$\heartsuit$ J 3
$\diamondsuit$ A K 7
$\clubsuit$ A 9 4

West leads the $\clubsuit$K against your Four Spades. You win the $\clubsuit$A and return a club at trick two, West winning as East discards a heart. West now switches to the $\heartsuit$K.

You seem to have only nine tricks – five trumps in hand and four top winners outside – so simply drawing trumps will not work, but your duplicated red-suit shape means that there are no ruffs to be taken in dummy. So, where might your tenth trick be found?

You were hoping to set up dummy's long club, despite the 4-1 split, but West's heart switch has prematurely removed a vital entry to dummy. Is it still possible to establish the thirteenth club and get back to cash it?

Let's see how the play might go: win the $\clubsuit$A and return a club. West wins and switches to the $\heartsuit$K. You win with the $\heartsuit$A and play a third round of clubs. West wins again, cashes the $\heartsuit$Q, and switches to the $\diamondsuit$J.

In order to both ruff the fourth round of clubs and to then reach the established club winner at the end, you need two more entries to dummy. Can you see how you might manage this?

The answer is to take a trump finesse – cash the $\spadesuit$K and then lead a low spade. When West follows low, insert dummy's $\spadesuit$9. If this wins and East follows suit, you can lead a fourth round of clubs and ruff it. You can then re-enter dummy with the ♠A, drawing the defenders' last trump in the process. Your diamond loser now disappears on the thirteenth club.

2.

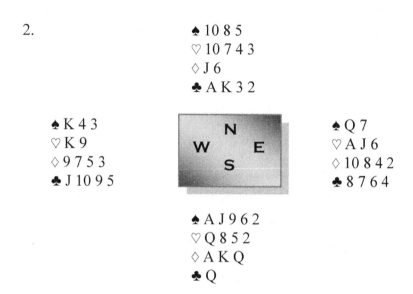

```
                        ♠ 10 8 5
                        ♡ 10 7 4 3
                        ◇ J 6
                        ♣ A K 3 2

♠ K 4 3              N                    ♠ Q 7
♡ K 9          W          E               ♡ A J 6
◇ 9 7 5 3           S                     ◇ 10 8 4 2
♣ J 10 9 5                                ♣ 8 7 6 4

                        ♠ A J 9 6 2
                        ♡ Q 8 5 2
                        ◇ A K Q
                        ♣ Q
```

West leads the ♣J against your spade game. Dummy is disappointing, to say the least. The good news, though, is that the defenders have not taken a heart ruff to beat you right out of the starting blocks. Can you see how to take advantage of that jot of good fortune and simultaneously justify your ambitious bidding?

The lack of obvious entries to dummy is a problem. We could win in dummy at trick one, smothering our ♣Q, in order to take one discard and then to lead a trump. Disposing of the fourth heart from our hand really doesn't help much, though. Can you spot a better solution?

This winning play here is only difficult to spot because of a smokescreen. Imagine for a moment that your ◇Q is, instead, a low diamond. How would you then play the hand?

Would it not then be fairly obvious to cash two high diamonds and follow by ruffing your losing diamond in dummy? Whilst on the table, you will be able to discard two heart losers on the high clubs before setting about trumps.

With East holding a doubleton honor in trumps, you will pick that suit up for one loser irrespective of how the defenders play. Ten tricks and contract made.

Now let's go back to the original layout. After winning the opening lead with the ♣Q, you should cash two diamond winners and then ruff the third round of the suit in dummy. That you are ruffing a winning diamond is irrelevant — you are just swapping tricks (one extra trump trick instead of a third diamond). What is vital, though, is that you get to dummy in order to access the discards on the high clubs and then to lead trumps through East.

3.

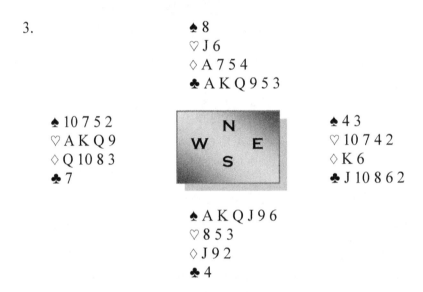

```
                          ♠ 8
                          ♡ J 6
                          ◊ A 7 5 4
                          ♣ A K Q 9 5 3

        ♠ 10 7 5 2              N              ♠ 4 3
        ♡ A K Q 9        W            E        ♡ 10 7 4 2
        ◊ Q 10 8 3             S              ◊ K 6
        ♣ 7                                    ♣ J 10 8 6 2

                          ♠ A K Q J 9 6
                          ♡ 8 5 3
                          ◊ J 9 2
                          ♣ 4
```

West leads three top hearts against your Four Spade game.

Faced with this problem at the table, you may be surprised by how many players would go down before they even began to think properly about how to play the hand. Having made it this far through this book, though, I confidently predict that you are not one of those.

What can possibly go wrong here? You have a solid enough trump suit and oodles of tricks.

The question I hope you are asking is "What does West lead at trick four?"

The answer is that it does not matter one jot what West leads after cashing his three heart winners provided, of course, that he is still on lead. Whatever he does, you will quickly be claiming ten tricks and your contract.

Anyone who ruffed the third round of hearts in dummy and then sat back to think about how to make a further nine tricks, though, will soon be discovering that they can no longer make their contract.

If declarer tries to cash three rounds of clubs to discard the two diamond losers, West will ruff the second club and play a diamond, ensuring one further trick for the defense. Declarer may, instead, try ruffing the second round of clubs with the nine, but West overruffs and plays a diamond, leading to two down. A third option is to ruff the second round of clubs high, but when declarer then tries to draw trumps, West shows up with a trump trick and again the contract has failed.

The thoughtful declarer, who asks "What can go wrong?" before doing anything committal, will appreciate that the key to this simple-looking deal is being able to get to hand to draw trumps. By discarding from dummy, rather than ruffing at trick three, you leave yourself with an answer to anything the defense might do.

4.

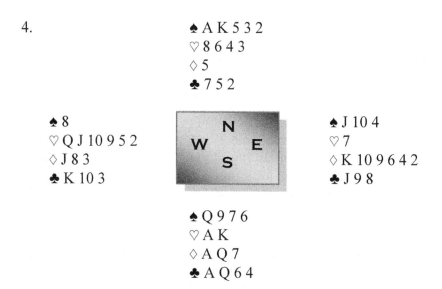

```
                    ♠ A K 5 3 2
                    ♡ 8 6 4 3
                    ◊ 5
                    ♣ 7 5 2

♠ 8                      N                ♠ J 10 4
♡ Q J 10 9 5 2      W         E           ♡ 7
◊ J 8 3                   S                ◊ K 10 9 6 4 2
♣ K 10 3                                  ♣ J 9 8

                    ♠ Q 9 7 6
                    ♡ A K
                    ◊ A Q 7
                    ♣ A Q 6 4
```

You declare Six Spades of the lead of the ♡Q.

Had you reached your slam in an uncontested auction, you might perhaps been tempted to try ruffing hearts in the short trump hand, but

West's opening bid has warned you that East is highly likely to hold a singleton in that suit. Your first priority, therefore, must be to remove East's trumps.

You start by cashing the ♠Q, then playing a second round of trumps to dummy hoping the suit will divide 2-2. When that fails, West discarding a heart, you have no choice but to draw a third round.

It now seems that the fate of your contract depends on finding East with the king of clubs and, even if that happens, you will probably also need the suit to split 3-3. That's a mere 18% chance: those don't seem like particularly favourable odds, do they?

Can you see how to boost your chances significantly?

You have two ace-queen combinations in the minors, so why rely on one finesse when you can take two? Which finesse should you take first, though? The answer is provided by the entry situation.

Play it through mentally to see what happens if you start by playing a club to the queen and it loses. Whether West returns a club or a heart after winning with the ♣K, you will be stuck in your hand. The only route back to dummy will be by cashing the ◇A and ruffing a diamond, which does not help at all.

Having drawn three rounds of trumps, you should take the diamond finesse at trick five.

If the queen of diamonds loses, you will need clubs to behave but, effectively, you will be no worse off than you were before. (You have one unavoidable club loser anyway, and you can now discard the third club from dummy on the ace of diamonds.)

When the diamond queen wins, you are most of the way home. You can now cash the ◇A, discarding dummy's third club, and ruff your last diamond to get back to dummy. Now, when you take the club finesse you have two ways to win: either the finesse wins or, if it loses you will be able to take advantage of a 3-3 club break by taking a ruff in dummy, establishing your long club as your twelfth trick.

Rather than relying on the club finesse and a 3-3 club break, you boost your chances significantly: this line of play is successful if either both minor-suit finesses win, or if one of them wins and the clubs split evenly: more than a 45% chance rather than under 20%.

Chapter 13 – The Endgame

We have so far looked at numerous methods of using the trump suit to generate extra tricks: establishing long-card tricks by ruffing is another way to achieve that objective. Here is a common side suit:

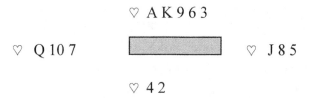

♡ AK963

♡ Q 10 7   ♡ J 8 5

♡ 4 2

With spades as trumps, you can cash the ace and king of hearts and then ruff the third round, bringing down the defenders' queen and jack, thus setting up two extra heart winners. All you then need is an outside entry to reach the North hand.

If the defenders' hearts are divided 4-2 you will need to ruff twice in order to establish one extra trick. To take two ruffs and get back to dummy to enjoy the thirteenth heart you will need two outside entries.

What about this side suit?

♣ K J 9 3

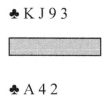

♣ A 4 2

This is a side suit that can produce anywhere from two to four tricks. The normal way to play the suit is to cash the ace and then to take a second-round finesse against the queen. If you are very lucky,

West will hold the queen and the suit will split 3-3, allowing you to score four tricks in the suit. (This will work less than one time in five, so beware of wagering the house on it.)

Sometimes, you need only to score three club tricks, and you can increase your chances of achieving that goal by first cashing the king, crossing to the ace, and then leading towards dummy's remaining doubleton jack. This line of play gives up the chance of making four club tricks and still scores three tricks any time that West holds the queen. The major difference, though, is that it also picks up a doubleton queen in the East hand.

Now suppose that you need to make three tricks from this suit, but without losing a club trick.

Essentially, it seems that you need West to hold the queen. What if you were able to discard a club from the South hand, though? Now you can succeed if either defender holds a doubleton queen or if the suit splits 3-3 (with the location of the queen irrelevant). Let's put this suit into a full deal:

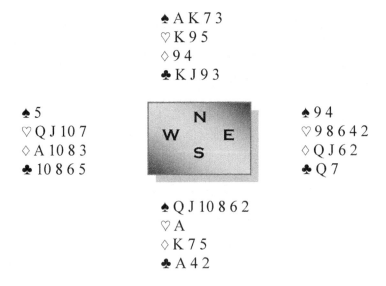

<pre>
               ♠ A K 7 3
               ♡ K 9 5
               ◊ 9 4
               ♣ K J 9 3

  ♠ 5   ♠ 9 4
  ♡ Q J 10 7   N   ♡ 9 8 6 4 2
  ◊ A 10 8 3   W   E   ◊ Q J 6 2
  ♣ 10 8 6 5   S   ♣ Q 7

               ♠ Q J 10 8 6 2
               ♡ A
               ◊ K 7 5
               ♣ A 4 2
</pre>

You bid unopposed to Six Spades and West leads the ♡Q.
How do you play?

You have ten tricks and potential losers in both minor suits, but there are multiple ways in which you might bring your trick tally of tricks to the required twelve.

If West holds Q-x-x in clubs, you can score four tricks in that suit via a finesse to add to six trumps and two hearts. If East holds the ace of diamonds, though, you can score two additional tricks with the ◇K and a diamond ruff.

The problem is that taking a losing finesse in one of the minors will sink your contract even though the other suit may lie favorably. So, how should you choose which minor to broach?

Playing for West to hold specifically three clubs to the queen is a long shot – it will work only about 18% of the time. A doubleton ♣10 with East would also allow you to score four tricks by finessing twice against West's queen. Even so, simply playing on diamonds offers much better odds as you need only to find the ace onside. Can you see a way to combine your chances in order to improve on those 50-50 odds?

Have you spotted the potential significance of dummy's third club, the nine?

The presence of the nine gives you an additional way in which you might score four club tricks and, more importantly, do so without risking a loser in the suit – by cashing the king and ace of clubs to see if the queen drops from the East hand. If it does so, you can then finesse against West's presumed ♣10 and subsequently discard two diamonds on the long club and the ♡K.

This is a completely free play: if the ♣Q does not fall from the East hand, you have lost nothing as you can still discard the third club from your hand on the ♡K and take the 50-50 shot of leading a diamond towards the king.

Although you will often start drawing trumps early in the deal, they can still be more than useful in numerous ways when it comes to the endgame. Perhaps you can use trumps to provide a vital entry, or to force a fatal discard out of a defender. They can also be used to hand the lead to a defender at a time when he least wants it.

See if you can spot the winning play in this game contract:

                    ♠ 7 3
                    ♡ Q 8 5 3
                    ◇ K 8 4 2
                    ♣ K 8 4

♠ Q J 10 9 8 2      ♠ 6 4
♡ K   ♡ J 10 9 4
◇ 9 6   ◇ Q 10 5
♣ Q 9 5 2   ♣ A 10 7 3

                    ♠ A K 5
                    ♡ A 7 6 2
                    ◇ A J 7 3
                    ♣ J 6

West opens the bidding with a weak two in spades and you quickly reach Four Hearts. West leads the ♠Q. How do you play?

After winning the opening spade lead, it looks right to start trumps immediately, and playing ace and another looks normal. When you cash the ♡A, though, there is both good news and bad, as West follows with the king, strongly suggesting that you have two unavoidable trump losers as well as the ace of clubs. There is no reason not to play a second round of trumps now, so you cross to the ♡Q, confirming the position.

It now seems that you will need some luck in both minors. You cannot afford to lose a diamond so the finesse in that suit will need to work: you cash the ◇K and play a diamond to the jack. The jack wins and you cash the ◇A next, removing East's exit card in that suit.

Now that East cannot profitably overruff dummy, it is time to eliminate spades: he follows when you cash your second winner in the suit and then throws a club as you ruff the third spade in dummy. When you lead the fourth round of diamonds, again East declines to ruff but he is only postponing the inevitable. You exit with a trump and East is left to lead away from his ♣A. The ♣K is your tenth trick.

On the previous deal, you had to make sure that the defender had no safe exit cards at the point he might have gained the lead. The actual end position, though, would have been equally effective in a notrump contract – the defender was thrown in to concede a trick by leading away from an honor.

An additional advantage of playing in a suit contract is that you can also force a defender on lead in a position where he has to concede a ruff-and-sluff. See if you can spot how Brazilian maestro Gabriel Chagas brought home his slam contract on this deal from the 2008 World Championships in Beijing:

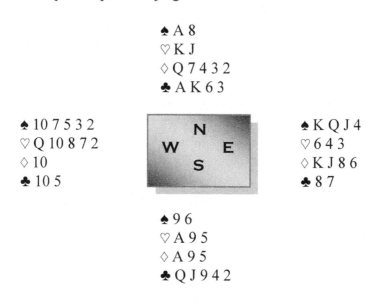

```
              ♠ A 8
              ♡ K J
              ◇ Q 7 4 3 2
              ♣ A K 6 3

♠ 10 7 5 3 2        N          ♠ K Q J 4
♡ Q 10 8 7 2    W       E      ♡ 6 4 3
◇ 10                S          ◇ K J 8 6
♣ 10 5                         ♣ 8 7

              ♠ 9 6
              ♡ A 9 5
              ◇ A 9 5
              ♣ Q J 9 4 2
```

With the vulnerable opponents silent, the Brazilians reached a poor Six Club contract from the South chair. West led a spade and the early play was predictable – win with the ♠A, play a trump to the queen and take a winning finesse of the heart jack. Declarer then cashed the ♡K, played a second trump to the jack, both defenders following, cashed the ♡A for a spade discard, and ruffed a spade in dummy.

Although this is not a great slam, the same contract was reached at a number of tables in Beijing and most declarers followed an identical line of play up to this point. All that now remained was to avoid two diamond losers. The mere mortals played a diamond to the ace and a second one back, conceding one down when West discarded.

The mercurial Brazilian led a diamond towards his hand and inserted the nine when East followed low. West won an unexpected trick with the ◇10 but had then to give a ruff-and-sluff: away went declarer's losing diamond. Just another routine +920! (It would be pedantic to point out that playing the ◊5 from hand is actually better than the nine, in case West began with J-10 doubleton.)

When I asked Gabriel Chagas later why he played this way, he observed that East seemed to hold strong spades but had not overcalled, suggesting he had only four spades and, thus, a balanced hand. East was, therefore, more likely to hold diamond length.

Note that if West holds the ◊K (so the 'normal' line of ace and another diamond works), the Chagas play will also succeeds, as West will be endplayed after winning the first round of diamonds cheaply. It is when West has to win with a singleton, as in the diagram, that the endplay collects all of the marbles.

How often have you mis-guessed trumps missing four cards including the queen? For those of us who have been playing for many years it is probably hundreds of times, if not thousands. With a little forethought, it is sometimes possible to play such a trump suit not caring whether you guess right or wrong. Take a look at this deal:

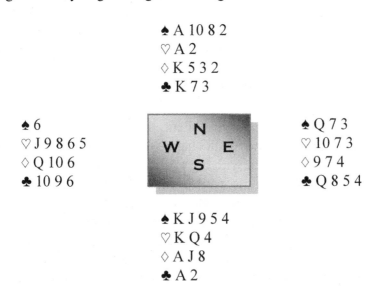

```
                    ♠ A 10 8 2
                    ♡ A 2
                    ◊ K 5 3 2
                    ♣ K 7 3

     ♠ 6                              ♠ Q 7 3
     ♡ J 9 8 6 5        N             ♡ 10 7 3
     ◊ Q 10 6      W         E        ◊ 9 7 4
     ♣ 10 9 6          S             ♣ Q 8 5 4

                    ♠ K J 9 5 4
                    ♡ K Q 4
                    ◊ A J 8
                    ♣ A 2
```

West leads the ♣10 against your contract of Six Spades. How do you play?

Losing to both pointed-suit queens would be unlucky. As long as East holds at least one trump, though, you can sidestep the trump guess entirely. Can you see how to make the contract with the diamond finesse losing irrespective of whether you guess the trumps?

Having won the opening lead in hand with the ♣K, you play a trump to the ace, both defenders following. The majority of declarers would now play a second trump, hoping to guess right and, if not, to fall back on the diamond finesse. There is a better option, though.

Let's see what happens if, instead, you play three rounds of hearts next, discarding dummy's low club. After then crossing to dummy with the ♣K, it is now time to play that second round of trumps. East follows with the remaining low trump and you can finesse the jack, not caring which defender holds the ♠Q.

If West discards on this trick, you can draw East's last trump and then take the diamond finesse for an overtrick. If the trump finesse loses to West's doubleton queen, he will then be endplayed either to give a ruff-and-sluff or to lead into your diamond tenace.

Had East discarded on the second round of trump, you would rise with the king and exit with a third trump to West's queen, again endplaying him to give you a twelfth trick.

Can you spot how to endplay an opponent into giving you a trick on our next deal? Remember that in a suit contract you will usually have at least one trump left in both your hand and dummy at the point when you throw the defender the lead:

```
              ♠ A 4
              ♡ Q 9 6 2
              ◊ A 7 4 2
              ♣ K 8 3

♠ 10 9 7 6 3 2      N        ♠ Q J 5
♡ 10            W       E    ♡ K J 4
◊ 9 6               S        ◊ Q 10 8 3
♣ J 9 6 4                    ♣ A Q 7

              ♠ K 8
              ♡ A 8 7 5 3
              ◊ K J 5
              ♣ 10 6 2
```

East opens with a strong (15-17 HCP) One Notrump and West (who is not playing transfers) removes himself to Two Spades. North doubles for takeout and your jump to Four Hearts ends a brief auction.

West leads the ♠10. How do you play?

The first question is where to win the opening lead.

With no obvious ruffs to take or long suits to establish, it seems clear to set about drawing trumps immediately. How do you intend to do so? With no opposition bidding, it would be normal to start with the ace of trumps followed by a second round towards dummy's queen, but that does not look like the right approach after East's opening bid. With East marked with both the ♡K and at least a doubleton in the suit, your best chance of avoiding more than one trump loser is to lead the queen from dummy. You should, therefore, win the opening lead in dummy with the ♠A.

At trick two you lead the ♡Q and East covers with the king. You win the ace, happily noting the fall of West's ♡10. You play a second round of trumps, West discarding as East wins with the ♡J. Note that you should be careful to manage your intermediate heart spots so that you retain the ability to move easily between your hand and dummy.

East exits with a second round of spades to your king. There is no reason not to draw the outstanding trump now, and you cross to dummy in the process in order to take the diamond finesse.

As expected, your ◊J wins the first round of that suit. With the ♣A marked in the East hand on the auction, it looks as if you need the defenders' diamonds to divide 3-3. Can you see how to make the contract even when diamonds fail to split evenly?

When you cash your top diamonds (ending in dummy), West discards a spade but you should still play the fourth round of the suit next. If you ruff this trick, you will go down. Instead, you should let East's ◊Q win while you discard one of your club losers. This card was never going to be a winner, so this is a classic loser-on-loser play.

East wins an unexpected diamond trick, but it is a poisoned chalice. With only black cards left, he has a choice of losing options – a third round of spades allows you to ruff in dummy whilst discarding a second club from your hand, and playing a club allows you to score a trick with the king. Either way, you will have ten tricks and your contract.

Trumps can occasionally be used in the endgame for more than just threatening a ruff-and-sluff. Indeed, how would you like to be declarer with two trump suits? Take a look at this deal:

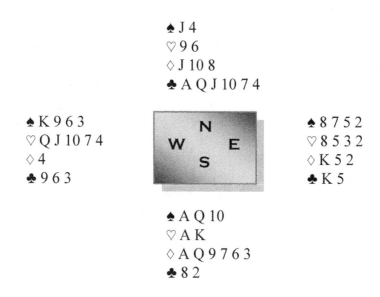

♠ J 4
♡ 9 6
◇ J 10 8
♣ A Q J 10 7 4

♠ K 9 6 3
♡ Q J 10 7 4
◇ 4
♣ 9 6 3

♠ 8 7 5 2
♡ 8 5 3 2
◇ K 5 2
♣ K 5

♠ A Q 10
♡ A K
◇ A Q 9 7 6 3
♣ 8 2

You bid unopposed to Six Diamonds and West leads the ♡Q. How do you play?

You have finesse positions in three suits but you would surely prefer to avoid having to take that many 50-50 gambles in a slam contract. Hopefully, dummy's clubs will at least enable you to avoid the spade finesse. The possible fly in the ointment, though, may be the lack of side suit entries to dummy's long suit.

You win the opening lead and immediately play a club to the queen. East grabs the king and exits with a second heart, putting you back in hand. Playing for West to hold the singleton king of trumps would be wildly against the odds, so you want to lead trumps from dummy. You will just have to hope that neither defender can ruff the second round of clubs.

So you cross to the ace of clubs and successfully run the jack of diamonds. You then call for the ten of diamonds. If East covers this, you will capture his king with your ace and then re-enter dummy with the $\diamond$8. Unfortunately, East follows with the last low diamond and West discards when you repeat the trump finesse.

If you draw the last trump at this point, then you will be stuck in your hand and the defense will eventually make the setting trick with the king of spades. It looks like you will have to stake your contract on the spade finesse after all – or does it?

How about using your second trump suit to nullify East's $\diamond$K? Indeed, from here you can guarantee success irrespective of how the defenders' card lie. What can East do if you simply lead a winning club from dummy? If he ruffs with his king, you will overruff and re-enter dummy with the third round of trumps. Your spades will then disappear on dummy's club winners. Of course, if East does not ruff the third round of clubs then you will simply discard a spade and lead another 'substitute trump' through him. Since trumping in produces the same result as before, East may allow that club trick to win too. Having disposed of all your potential spade losers, you can now simply draw the last trump and claim your slam.

Quiz Hands

1.   ♠ Q 7 5 4 2
                           ♡ 9 6
                           ◇ A 6 5
                           ♣ K 9 3

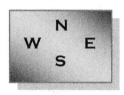

                     ♠ A 8
                     ♡ A K Q 7 4 3
                     ◇ 4
                     ♣ A Q J 7

You reach Six Hearts in an uncontested auction.
West leads the ◇Q.
How do you play?

2.

♠ A 8 4
♡ 9 6
♢ 10 6 5
♣ 9 7 6 4 3

♠ K Q J 7 5 3
♡ 7 3
♢ A Q 4
♣ A Q

West	North	East	South
—	—	1♡	Dbl
3♡	Pass	Pass	3♠
Pass	4♠	All Pass	

West leads the ♡K and a second heart to East's ace. East then exits with a trump to your king. You play a second trump to dummy's ace on which East pitches a heart.

How should you continue?

1.
           ♠ Q 7 5 4 2
           ♡ 9 6
           ◇ A 6 5
           ♣ K 9 3

♠ K J 3   ♠ 10 9 6
♡ J 10 8 2   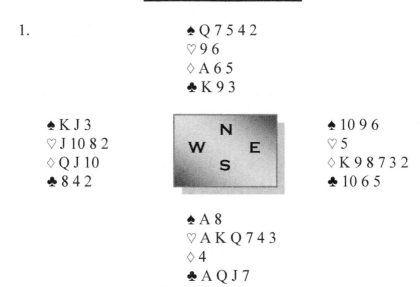   ♡ 5
◇ Q J 10   ◇ K 9 8 7 3 2
♣ 8 4 2   ♣ 10 6 5

           ♠ A 8
           ♡ A K Q 7 4 3
           ◇ 4
           ♣ A Q J 7

You reach Six Hearts in an uncontested auction and West opens the defense with the ◇Q.

On the surface, it seems that you have an unavoidable spade loser so the fate of your contract will depend on the trumps dividing 3-2. There are no ruffs to be taken in the short trump hand and no long suits to be developed, so is there any reason why you should not simply win the ◇A and draw trumps? Indeed, most players would be in such a hurry to cash a couple of trump winners and claim when everyone followed that they would think no further about the deal. When East discards on the second round of trumps, they would shrug their shoulders, bemoan their bad luck, and move on to the next deal without even realizing that they should have made this contract.

If there is a trump loser, then the only realistic chance of making the contract (other than finding the ♠K singleton is to endplay a defender into leading away from the ♠K. At the time when you throw the defender in, though, he will need to be left with only spades. It is therefore essential that you do everything you can to remove any safe exit cards he may have.

To do this, you must make use of both entries to dummy. You are in dummy for the first time at trick one after winning the ◇A, so you need to ruff a diamond immediately. Having done that, you can now lay down your top trumps. East shows out on the second round, but you are still in the ballgame. Cross to the ♣K and ruff another diamond. Now start cashing your club winners. West can ruff the fourth club with his trump trick, but will be left with only spades to play. Failing to ruff only delays the agony for him – you exit with your last trump at trick eleven, and West is forced to lead away from his ♠K at the death: slam made.

2.

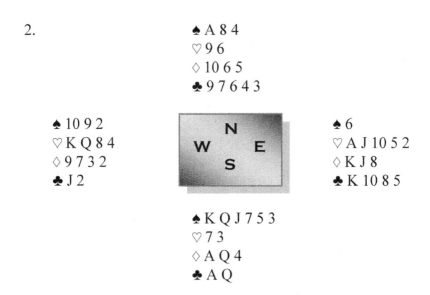

♠ A 8 4
♡ 9 6
◇ 10 6 5
♣ 9 7 6 4 3

♠ 10 9 2
♡ K Q 8 4
◇ 9 7 3 2
♣ J 2

♠ 6
♡ A J 10 5 2
◇ K J 8
♣ K 10 8 5

♠ K Q J 7 5 3
♡ 7 3
◇ A Q 4
♣ A Q

You reach Four Spades and West leads the ♡K and a second heart to East's ace. East then exits with a trump to your king. You play a second trump to dummy's ace on which East pitches a heart.

West has already shown up with the king and queen of hearts, so it is almost certain that both minor-suit finesses are working. The problem, though, is that you have only one obvious entry to dummy, so how are you going to take them both?

If trumps had split 2-2, you could have accessed dummy for a second time with the ♠8, but with West still holding the ten of trumps that is not an option.

Let's say you make use of the entry to play a diamond to East's ten and your queen, which wins. You then try cashing all of your trumps. East discards two more hearts, the ◇J and a club. Hoping that East is now down to K-9 in diamonds and K-x in clubs, you play ace and another diamond hoping to endplay him. Unfortunately, West wins the third round of diamonds with the nine and, to add insult to injury, cashes two red suit winners to defeat you by two tricks.

The idea of an endplay was the right one. See that happens, though, if you cash the ◊A and immediately exit with a third round of diamonds, without drawing the last trump: East has not been able to rid himself of the ◊J so he is forced to win and he has no good exit. If he plays a heart for a ruff-and-sluff, you will ruff in dummy and throw the CQ. If he plays a club, he gives you the finesse.

Chapter 14 – Timing

Having seen plenty of defensive prods race to the boundary, cricket aficionados will understand the importance of timing. A lazy-looking but perfectly-timed drive can send a golf ball further than seems possible. When declaring at bridge, timing is equally important, both in notrumps and suit play. Indeed, this book could have been entitled 'timing', since the underlying feature has been 'when to draw trumps'. Here, though, we look at some deals on which you act early in order to prepare for an end position that makes use of the trump suit.

We start with a deal at which, having ploughed through this far, you may scoff. It has defeated many of my students, though, so let's see how you fare. Cover the E/W cards and see if you would bring home your game contract:

♠ K 8 6 3
♡ Q 4 2
◇ 7
♣ A K 8 5 2

♠ J 9 5   ♠ Q 10
♡ K 8 3   ♡ 10 9 6 5
◇ Q J 10 5 2   ◇ A 9 4
♣ J 6   ♣ Q 10 9 3

♠ A 7 4 2
♡ A J 7
◇ K 8 6 3
♣ 7 4

You reach Four Spades uncontested and West leads the ◇Q. East wins with the ◇A and returns a diamond. How do you play?

Declarer is in a 4-4 trump fit with no intermediates and, as is often the case on hands of this type, the problem is one of timing. First, count your losers from declarer's hand: one in trumps (assuming a 3-2 break), one in hearts and three in diamonds (after the lead). There is no skullduggery required here -- there is a straightforward solution: simply reduce those five losers to the required three by ruffing two of your diamond losers in dummy.

The key here is how many rounds of trumps to play. With trump holdings like this spade suit, you generally want to draw precisely two rounds of trumps before taking ruffs. Indeed, that is the case here. If you start ruffing diamonds in dummy without drawing two rounds of trumps first, East will score an overruff with the short trump holding and you will still have two tricks to lose to West. What you cannot afford to do, though, is to draw three rounds of trumps, for then you will have only one trump in dummy for two losing diamonds.

'But I wouldn't draw three rounds of trumps', you say. Let's see what might happen: suppose you win the ◊K, cash two top trumps, and then take your first diamond ruff. You then notice that you need to take a finesse to establish your second heart winner, so you try to return to your hand by playing a heart to the jack. What happens now is that West wins with the ♡K and draws a third round of trumps. You will eventually lose a second diamond trick – one down.

This is an easy hand provided you think the whole thing through before you play. There are two possible lines of play. Win the ◊K, draw one round of trumps as you cross to dummy with the ♠K, and then play a heart to the jack. Whatever happens, you will be able to draw a second round of trumps, cash your heart and club winners, and crossruff the remaining tricks in the minors. West can ruff or overruff one trick with his master trump, but you will take the remainder.

Alternatively, you can play low from hand at trick two and ruff the second round of diamonds in dummy. Now you can afford to cash two high trumps (ending in your hand) and lead your last diamond loser to ruff in dummy. A heart to the jack establishes your second trick in that suit. West can cash his trump winner but your hand is now high.

Our next deal takes us back to a theme we visited in a very early chapter — ruffing losers in the short trump hand. The process is not always as straightforward as it seems.

♠ K 6 4 2
♡ A 4
◇ A 7 5
♣ K 9 4 2

♠ A Q J 5 3
♡ 7 5 2
◇ K 8 6
♣ Q 5

With both sides vulnerable, West opens with a weak Two Heart bid. You soon find yourself in Four Spades and West leads the ♡J. How do you play?

You can count five trumps plus three top winners in the red suits. A club trick can be developed by force to bring your total to nine. You still need to find one more trick from somewhere, but this looks easy enough as you can ruff your third heart in dummy. The answer to the question "If I draw trumps, will I have enough tricks for my contract?" appears to be "Yes". Even though you need to score a ruff to bring your total to the required number, you can probably do so after drawing trumps: there is no rush to take your heart ruff.

The correct play is to win the opening lead with the ♡A and play a trump to hand. If both defenders follow suit, you can then draw the remaining trumps, concede a heart, and subsequently score your tenth trick by ruffing your third heart in dummy.

At one of the tables where I saw this hand played, declarer won the opening heart lead with the ace and immediately returned a second heart. West overtook his partner's ♡Q and continued with the ♡10.

Our hero was sufficiently astute to realize from the bidding that East was now out of hearts, so he ruffed with the king. Most of the time, this would be okay, but this was not declarer's lucky day. Here is the full deal:

                    ♠ K 6 4 2
                    ♡ A 4
                    ◇ A 7 5
                    ♣ K 9 4 2

♠ ---   ♠ 10 9 8 7
♡ K J 10 8 6 3   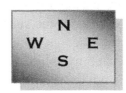   ♡ Q 5
◇ J 9 2   ◇ Q 10 4 3
♣ A 10 6 3   ♣ J 8 7

                    ♠ A Q J 5 3
                    ♡ 7 5 2
                    ◇ K 8 6
                    ♣ Q 5

When declarer belatedly played the first round of trumps, West discarded. East now held a natural trump trick and declarer had to lose a trick in each suit – one down.

Suppose, instead, that you check the trump position by playing one round before conceding the heart: win the ♡A and play a spade to your ace. When West shows out, you realize that the plan to draw trumps before ruffing your heart will not now work as dummy will then have no trump left. There was nothing wrong with your original plan, but occasionally bad breaks will mean that you need to reassess.

Seeing nothing better to do at this stage, perhaps you now continue by a conceding a heart to West. When he continues with a third round of the suit, you know that you will go down if you ruff this with the king, so instead you ruff low, forlornly hoping that East might have to follow suit after all. Alas, East overruffs and, as before, you end up losing a trick in each suit. Still one down! So what can be done?

As you probably realize by now, you cannot make this contract by ruffing a heart in dummy. Ruffing low allows East to score one of his trumps by overruffing. Ruffing high promotes East's trumps into a natural trick. How, then, can you manufacture a tenth trick?

The answer is that you must ruff a diamond in dummy!

This may look rather unlikely when you first look at the deal, but once you spot the solution it is not so difficult to understand. The reason you cannot score a heart ruff is that East is also short in that suit. You have to lose a diamond trick anyway, so it costs nothing to discard dummy's third diamond on the third round of hearts!

How will the play go? Win the ♡A and play a trump to the ace, getting the bad news. Now play a second heart but throw a diamond from dummy when West continues the suit. If West now switches to a diamond, you can win the ace, cross to the ◊K and play a third diamond, ruffing low in dummy while East must follow suit. Now draw trumps and lead a club to establish your tenth trick. (If West plays a fourth round of hearts rather than switching to diamonds, you can ruff low in dummy. If East overruffs, you overruff him and you have effectively drawn a second round of trumps. You still have one low trump in dummy with which to ruff the third round of diamonds.)

On our next deal, declarer at the table was scared by phantoms and so managed to fail to the simply mundane. Cover the E/W cards to see if you can chalk up this slam:

N/S Vul: Dealer North

```
              ♠ ---
              ♡ A 8 4 3
              ◊ A J 9 5 3
              ♣ K J 9 2

♠ K 7 5              N              ♠ A J 10 9 6 4 2
♡ 10 9 6 5      W         E         ♡ K 7
◊ K 6 4              S              ◊ 8 2
♣ 7 4 3                             ♣ 6 5

              ♠ Q 8 3
              ♡ Q J 2
              ◊ Q 10 7
              ♣ A Q 10 8
```

West	North	East	South
—	1◊	3♠	Dbl
4♠	4NT	Pass	5♣
Pass	6♣	All Pass	

East makes a pre-emptive bid in spades and West raises him to game. You do well to reach slam, and choose the 4-4 club fit rather than the alternative minor suit, where a forcing game by the defense would prove successful if trumps failed to break evenly.

West leads the ♠5 against your Six Club contract and you ruff in dummy. You get off to a good start by playing a trump to your hand and leading the ◊Q, covered by king and ace. How should you now continue?

When the deal was played at the table, declarer was worried by the possibility of a second-round diamond ruff after the opponents' pre-emption. Our hero therefore drew the remaining trumps ending in his hand and ran the ♡Q, banking his contract on the finesse into the pre-emptor (the hand likely to be short in hearts).

When this lost to East's king, the defenders were able to cash spade tricks to set the contract by two.

Declarer had the right idea, but his timing was awry. He could afford to lose a trick to the ♡K, but he must arrange to take the finesse when losing it would not prove immediately fatal to the contract. Rather than drawing all of the outstanding trumps, he should have re-entered his hand with a second round of clubs and taken the heart finesse while dummy still had a trump to protect against a spade continuation.

Yes, he would still have gone down if the heart finesse lost and West held the missing trump and no more diamonds, but those are significantly better odds than simply relying on the success of the heart finesse alone.

One other point worth noting is which diamond declarer should lead at trick three: the ◊10 is significantly better than the queen. Why? Because West may cover the queen hoping to promote the ten in his partner's hand. He cannot afford to cover the ten, though, lest his partner holds the singleton queen.

Note also that East cannot afford to duck the king if the finesse is wrong – after all, might declarer not play this way with a doubleton ten and no queen? So, you find out that the finesse is working and you also know that West still has at least one diamond. (Indeed, if he does cover the ten with the king, there is a very good chance that he started with a singleton.)

The three most important aspects of successful declarer play are (with apologies to Tony Blair) planning, planning and planning. Even if your play to trick one is automatic, you should still stop to formulate a plan before calling for that first card from the dummy. The easiest way to make your plan is to project the play:

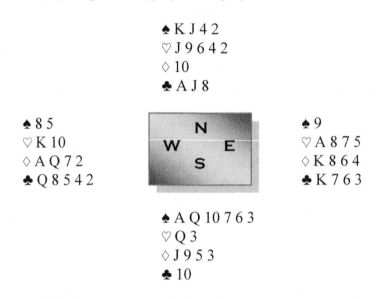

As Dealer with both sides vulnerable, you open with a weak two in spades and your partner raises to game. West leads a trump. How do you play?

When the deal arose at the table, declarer saw the singleton diamond in the short trump hand and thought no further than that. He won the opening lead in dummy and immediately led the ◊10. West won with the queen and continued with a second trump. Declarer won in hand, ruffed a diamond, returned to his hand by ruffing the second round of clubs, and took a second diamond ruff.

Having exhausted dummy of trumps, declarer was still left with three more losers (one diamond and two hearts), so the contract was one down. Had declarer projected the play before committing himself, he would have realized that there were not enough trumps in dummy to enable him to ruff all of his diamond losers. Perhaps, then, he would have seen that it was possible to make ten tricks by using dummy's moderate heart suit.

Suppose declarer wins the opening trump lead in his hand and leads a low heart. If West plays low, declarer intends to finesse dummy's nine. If this forces a high honor from East, declarer will later be able to establish a heart winner by force. As the defensive cards lie, with West holding K-10 doubleton, declarer's play will bear immediate fruit.

However, I only gave you the queen, jack and nine of hearts in an attempt to make it more obvious that declarer could establish a heart trick In fact, if I had given you 3-2 of hearts opposite 8-7-6-5-4 it would still be correct to win the opening trump lead in hand to play a heart. There are sufficient entries to dummy (the ♣A and two diamond ruffs) to set up and reach the fifth heart provided the suit splits no worse than 4-2.

As declarer, you should always remember the auction since it will often reveal important clues about the defenders' hands, either their distribution, the location of the missing high cards, or both. See if you can use that hint to bring home your game contract on our next deal:

Neither Vul: Dealer West

```
              ♠ K 7 4 3
              ♡ 8 6 4 3 2
              ◇ J 6
              ♣ 9 2
♠ Q 9 8 5              N            ♠ J 10 2
♡ A K Q 10       W         E        ♡ J 9 7 5
◇ A 10 2              S            ◇ K 9 8 5 4
♣ J 7                               ♣ 6
              ♠ A 6
              ♡ ---
              ◇ Q 7 3
              ♣ A K Q 10 8 5 4 3
```

West	North	East	South
1NT	Pass	2♣	5♣
All Pass			

229

West opens with a strong (15-17 HCP) One Notrump and East makes a Stayman inquiry. Your jump to Five Clubs then ends the brief auction.

West leads the ♡K. How do you play?

You have ten tricks and the objective is, therefore, to avoid losing three diamonds. West's opening bid marks him with most of the missing high cards, so perhaps you decide to draw trumps and lead towards dummy's ◊J, hoping to find West with both the ace and king. Is there not a chance, though, that West would have led a diamond if he held both high honors?

It looks like you will need to take a diamond ruff in order to bring your trick tally up to eleven. Perhaps then, you elect to play a diamond towards the jack after ruffing the opening lead:

When East beats the ◊J with his king and returns a trump you are in trouble. You play a second diamond, but West wins and plays a second round of trumps, denuding dummy and leaving you with a third loser at the end.

So, what can be done?

There is one more significant clue left to be gained from the bidding. What do you make of East's Stayman bid? You know that he does not hold enough values to invite game and this suggests that he was intending to pass his partner's response to Stayman, whatever it was. This means that he is likely to hold diamond length and, significantly, short clubs.

West's notrump opening also strongly suggests that he will hold at least two trumps. To succeed, you must therefore make West win the first round of diamonds.

How can you do that?

Note the difference if you ruff the heart lead and cross to dummy with the ♠K at trick two. When you then play a diamond, East cannot afford to win with the king or you will be able to make a diamond trick by force with your jack-queen combination. Your ◊Q therefore loses to West's ace and he plays a trump. However, when you now play a second diamond to the jack and East's king he has no trump.

Despite the earlier reminder to listen carefully to the auction, do not allow yourself to be blinded (deafened?) by it. On our next deal, declarer based his line of play on an assumption drawn from the auction when there was no need to do so. When that assumption turned out to be false, his contract bit the dust:

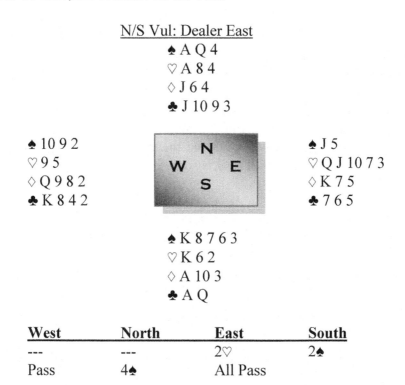

N/S Vul: Dealer East

♠ A Q 4
♡ A 8 4
◇ J 6 4
♣ J 10 9 3

♠ 10 9 2
♡ 9 5
◇ Q 9 8 2
♣ K 8 4 2

♠ J 5
♡ Q J 10 7 3
◇ K 7 5
♣ 7 6 5

♠ K 8 7 6 3
♡ K 6 2
◇ A 10 3
♣ A Q

West	North	East	South
---	---	2♡	2♠
Pass	4♠	All Pass	

East takes advantage of the favourable vulnerability to open with a weak two bid in hearts as dealer. You overcall Two Spades on your rather moth-eaten suit and soon find yourself in game.

West leads the ♡9 against your Four Spades. What is your plan?

At the table, declarer won the opening lead in hand with the ♡K and started trumps by cashing dummy's ace and queen. When both defenders followed suit, everything looked rosy in declarer's garden.

Taking advantage of the entry to dummy, declarer next played a club and finessed the queen. When West won with the ♣K and was able to produce an unexpected second heart to remove dummy's final entry, though, declarer found himself with four unavoidable losers.

Declarer bemoaned the fact that he had been fooled by East's opening weak two bid on only a 5-card suit, but does his explanation hold water?

231

In fact, the contract was cold once both defenders followed to the second round of trumps and declarer's line of play was simply careless. He can ensure ten tricks irrespective of how the defenders' hearts are distributed by simply drawing the last trump and then leading the ace and queen of clubs from his hand. Indeed, West must allow declarer's ♣Q to win in order to save the overtrick – if he takes the king then declarer can then discard two red-suit losers on dummy's jack and ten of clubs.

Is this the best line of play, though? Suppose, instead, that the trumps do not split, as will often be the case when an opponent has pre-empted. Perhaps the full deal is something like:

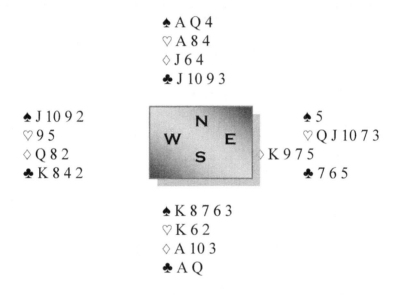

♠ A Q 4
♡ A 8 4
◇ J 6 4
♣ J 10 9 3

♠ J 10 9 2
♡ 9 5
◇ Q 8 2
♣ K 8 4 2

♠ 5
♡ Q J 10 7 3
◇ K 9 7 5
♣ 7 6 5

♠ K 8 7 6 3
♡ K 6 2
◇ A 10 3
♣ A Q

As novices, we all learned that when we have a suit such as the spades on this deal we should cash the suit by playing the honors in the short holding first (to prevent blocking the suit). That's all very well and is a sound general principle, but you need to be able to work out when to break such rules due to the requirements of the deal as a whole.

Lacking any intermediates in the spade suit, there is no way to avoid a trump loser if the suit splits 4-1. With four potential losers in the side suits too, you are going to need to score three club tricks on this deal, so entries to dummy must be preserved. Rather than winning the first two rounds of trumps with dummy's ace and queen, you should instead intentionally block the suit by winning with your ♠K and one of dummy's honors. It is then time to start on clubs, and without finessing! Play the ♣A and then the ♣Q. As before, West does best to duck his king of clubs, but doing so will not help him since you still have two entries to dummy.

Now is the time to draw the third round of trumps, simultaneously crossing to dummy with that carefully preserved honor. You can now lead the ♣J from dummy and discard a diamond from your hand. West wins with the ♣K now and he can choose to cash his trump winner or not. Either way, you are going to be able to throw another red-suit loser on dummy's established ♣10. You will lose just one trump, one club and one red-suit trick.

Our next deal looks deceptively simple, and yet I would wager that if it was played at a large number of tables most declarers would go down. Many would shrug their shoulders, comment that there was nothing they could do, and go on to the next deal without thinking any more about it. Principles such as "take ruffs", "draw trumps", "lead towards honors" are drilled into everyone whilst in their bridge cradles, but sometimes a play that is counter-intuitive is required. This time you are even welcome to look at all four hands to see if you can spot how you must play to bring home your contract:

♠ K 9 5 3
♡ K J 6
◇ K 5
♣ A Q 8 4

♠ A 8 6
♡ 9 8 6 2
◇ J 9 2
♣ J 10 6

♠ Q 4
♡ 3
◇ Q 10 7 6 4
♣ K 9 7 5 2

♠ J 10 7 2
♡ A Q 10 7 5
◇ A 8 3
♣ 3

You reach Four Hearts after an uncontested auction and West leads the ♣J. How would you play?

Does it not look obvious to begin by ruffing a diamond in dummy, then drawing trumps and establishing the spades? If you mentally play the hand through before committing yourself, you will discover that this line of play is fraught with danger.

Let's see how the play might go: you win the ♣A, cash the high diamonds and ruff a diamond with dummy's low trump. You cash the king of hearts but when you then lead the second round of trumps from dummy East discards a club. Fortunately, your suit is just strong enough so that you can overtake and draw West remaining trumps.

Now you lead the ♠J and West follows with a low card. With no opposition bidding to suggest how the spade honors might lie, you guess to run the jack. East wins with the ♠Q and continues with the ◊Q. You discard a spade in the hope that diamonds will split 4-4 and the defense will have to give you something on the next trick, but West discards a spade and East continues with a fifth round of diamonds. You ruff with your last trump and lead a spade perforce. West wins with the ace and leads a club to his partner's king: one down.

"I had to guess the spades right once the trumps split 4-1", you comment as partner nods sagely and commiserates with you. It was all very unfortunate. Or was it?

When you counted your tricks before playing to trick one, how many did you come to? Five trumps in hand, the ♣A, two top diamonds and a diamond ruff – nine. So, how many spade tricks did you need?

The answer is one and, indeed, you can even afford to lose three spade tricks – the ace, the queen and a ruff. The correct play is to win the ♣A, cash one high trump from dummy, and then to lead a low spade!

No matter what the defenders now do, you are in control. Indeed, as the cards lie in the diagram above you will end up with twelve tricks unless East is clairvoyant. (If he does not rise with the ♠Q when you lead the low spade from dummy at trick three, your jack will force West's ace. When you then play a second round of spades later in the hand, you will know that the queen is offside so you will play to the king and East's queen will drop.)

Our final deal requires you to take a finesse and execute an endplay, but I'd wager that faced with the situation at the table the majority of players would fail to make their contract. As an additional clue, I give you fair warning that there are more finesses available here than may appear at first glance. Feel free to look at all four hands:

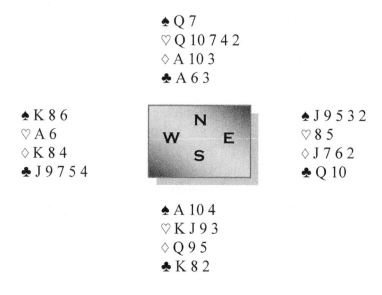

♠ Q 7
♡ Q 10 7 4 2
◇ A 10 3
♣ A 6 3

♠ K 8 6
♡ A 6
◇ K 8 4
♣ J 9 7 5 4

♠ J 9 5 3 2
♡ 8 5
◇ J 7 6 2
♣ Q 10

♠ A 10 4
♡ K J 9 3
◇ Q 9 5
♣ K 8 2

You reach what looks like a normal Four Heart contract against which West leads the ♣5. How do you play?

You seem to have a loser in each suit. Which loser do you suppose can be avoided?

The only possibility is to establish a second spade trick in order to discard dummy's third club. The club lead makes the situation urgent, though, which means that you must play on spades before knocking out the ace of trumps. There are also entry problems – you have only one fast entry to your hand.

Let's see what happens if you win the opening club lead with the king and lead a spade towards dummy's queen. West rises with the ♠K and perhaps you think that your finesse has now succeeded. The spades, though, are blocked. You can win West's club continuation with dummy's ace and cash the ♠Q but you then have no route back to your hand to enable you to cash the ♠A before the defenders can cash their club winner.

Can you see how to avoid this blockage?

What if I told you that the position of the ♠K is irrelevant?

The answer is indeed to take a spade finesse, but against the jack!

Suppose, for a moment, that East had held both king and jack of spades. Dummy's queen would have lost to East's king on the first round of the suit, but you would then have taken a finesse against East's presumed jack on the second round of spades in order to establish a second winner in the suit.

But West holds the ♠K, you may be thinking. Indeed he does, but look what happens if you play dummy's ♠Q under the king: West continues clubs to dummy's ace and you can now finesse against the jack of spades. When the ♠10 wins the second round of the suit you are conveniently in hand to cash the ♠A and discard dummy's losing club. You can now ruff a club in dummy (with a high trump) as East discards a spade, and set about playing trumps.

West wins the first round of trumps with the ace and exits with a second round, East following suit. All you now need to do is to avoid losing two diamond tricks. These cards remain:

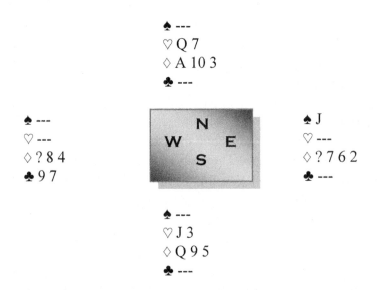

You did remember to win the trumps exit in your hand, didn't you? Breaching diamonds from dummy leaves either with a nasty guess whether you start with the ace or a low card. If, instead, you lead towards dummy's diamonds, inserting the ten when West does not play an honor, your contract is guaranteed irrespective of the position. Even if East wins cheaply with the jack, he will then be endplayed either to return a diamond, your queen-nine ensuring that the king is neutralized no matter who holds it) or to concede a ruff-and-sluff.

Quiz Hands

1.

      ♠ K Q 10 8
      ♡ K 7 3
      ◇ A
      ♣ K Q 7 6 2

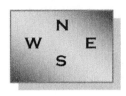

      ♠ A 7 5 3
      ♡ Q 4 2
      ◇ Q 10 5
      ♣ 8 5 3

You bid unopposed to Four Spades.
West leads the ♡J, your queen winning. How should you continue?

2.

      ♠ K Q 4
      ♡ J 3
      ◇ 9 6 3
      ♣ 10 8 7 6 2

      ♠ A J 7 5 3
      ♡ A K
      ◇ A J 10 8
      ♣ J 3

You reach Four Spades uncontested.
West leads the ♡10. How do you play?

Answers to Quiz Hands

1.

```
                    ♠ K Q 10 8
                    ♡ K 7 3
                    ◇ A
                    ♣ K Q 7 6 2

♠ 6 4                    N              ♠ J 9 2
♡ J 10 9 6        W          E          ♡ A 8 5
◇ K J 7 6              S                ◇ 9 8 4 3 2
♣ A 10 4                               ♣ J 9

                    ♠ A 7 5 3
                    ♡ Q 4 2
                    ◇ Q 10 5
                    ♣ 8 5 3
```

Against your Four Spades, West leads the ♡J, which is ducked around to your queen.

Throughout this book, we have established the general principle that it is usually right to draw trumps if you do not need to score ruffing tricks. We have also observed that drawing trumps is generally a good idea if you have winners in a long suit that the opponents might ruff. These 'rules' both suggest that you should start by drawing trumps immediately here, so is this the correct thing to do?

The problem with general rules, of course, is that you need to be able to recognize when to break them, and this hand is an example of such an occasion. It looks as if you probably have two heart losers (although there is a chance that East might hold the doubleton ace). If you do have two hearts to lose, though, you will need to restrict your club losers to one. To give you the best chance of doing this, you will need to lead clubs twice from your hand. You are in hand now, after trick one, and you have only one more entry.

Yes, the defenders might be able to take a club ruff if you play the suit right away, without drawing trumps, but ask yourself whether you are going to make the contract by any other route if the clubs split 4-1. The answer, you will find, is 'no'.

Essentially, you need to find West with either a doubleton or tripleton ace of clubs to make the hand legitimately. In reality, though, you will also prevail most of the time when East holds a low singleton club too. (It will not be obvious to West that he must rise with the ♣A at trick two, continue with the ♡10 and, when that holds, play a club for his partner to ruff.) So, play a club at trick two. Assuming that the ♣K wins in dummy, you can now draw trumps ending in your hand in order to lead a second round of clubs.

Note also that the 'normal' method of playing this spade suit in isolation would be to cash one high honor from dummy and then to play a second round to the ace, enabling you to pick up four to the jack in the West hand. On this deal, though, you cannot afford to adopt this line since you need to use the only remaining entry to hand to lead a second club towards dummy, so you might just as well play on the assumption that the trumps are going to divide 3-2.

2.

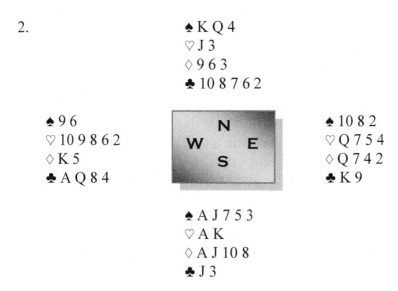

```
                        ♠ K Q 4
                        ♡ J 3
                        ◇ 9 6 3
                        ♣ 10 8 7 6 2

  ♠ 9 6                                      ♠ 10 8 2
  ♡ 10 9 8 6 2          N                    ♡ Q 7 5 4
  ◇ K 5            W          E              ◇ Q 7 4 2
  ♣ A Q 8 4             S                    ♣ K 9

                        ♠ A J 7 5 3
                        ♡ A K
                        ◇ A J 10 8
                        ♣ J 3
```

You bid unopposed to Four Spades and West leads the ♡10.

The most common reason to delay drawing trumps is because you need to take ruffs in the short trump hand. That is clearly not the case here, but you still cannot afford to draw trumps immediately since you will then be left with two losers in each minor.

Clearly, you would prefer to play diamonds at least twice from dummy, and you must therefore use your trump entries to do so. Win the heart lead and play two rounds of trumps ending in dummy (and leaving dummy with a high trump). Now play a diamond and put in the ten or jack from hand. Note: DO NOT waste either dummy's ◇9 by leading it on the first round of the suit or the eight in your hand, both of which you may need later.

West wins the first diamond with the king, but when you regain the lead you can re-enter dummy with the third round of trumps. Now is the time to lead the ◇9, underplaying with the carefully-preserved eight from your hand if East follows low so that the lead remains in dummy so you can lead a third round from there if necessary. Provided East was dealt at least one of the diamond honors, you will make your contract no matter how the suit divides.

I hope you have found this book both instructive and entertaining. I look forward to seeing you at the table. M.S.